SECRETS OF A BACK-ALLEY
ID MAN

SECRETS OF A BACK-ALLEY ID MAN

Fake ID Construction Techniques of the Underground

Sheldon Charrett

Paladin Press
Boulder, Colorado

Also by Sheldon Charrett:

Electronic Circuits and Secrets of an Old-Fashioned Spy
Identity, Privacy, and Personal Freedom
The Modern Identity Changer

Secrets of a Back-Alley ID Man:
Fake ID Construction Techniques of the Underground
by Sheldon Charrett

Copyright © 2001 by Sheldon Charrett

ISBN 1-58160-268-5
Printed in the United States of America

Published by Paladin Press, a division of
Paladin Enterprises, Inc.
Gunbarrel Tech Center
7077 Winchester Circle
Boulder, Colorado 80301 USA
+1.303.443.7250

Direct inquiries and/or orders to the above address.

PALADIN, PALADIN PRESS, and the "horse head" design
are trademarks belonging to Paladin Enterprises and
registered in United States Patent and Trademark Office.

Visit our Web site at: www.paladin-press.com

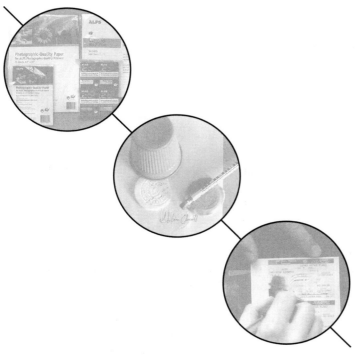

Table of Contents

ACKNOWLEDGEMENTS

I wish to acknowledge the following individuals for their contributions to this work. In no particular order, I extend thanks to the following:

- Shane McAndrews. He knows why.
- Pauline. She knows why.
- Jane Smith. For sharing all her informative tidbits and thought experiments and for printing out my PVC templates. Thanks for the Joyride.
- Bill P. For his invaluable information on PVC card construction and diffractive films. Thanks for the templates.
- SwitcherX. For hooking me up.
- George. For his boldness in getting the discussion forum under way.
- Peder, Jon, and the Paladin gang. For 30 years of carrying the torch, publishing books on controversial subjects so ordinary citizens could share this information. For continuing to carry the torch on all subjects not yet banned by our government.
- What's left of the First Amendment to the Constitution of the United States of America. Thanks for hanging in there, First Amendment. You've taken a beating in recent years. Yet, though you are dazed, confused, and barely able to keep your balance, you are somehow still standing. I will miss you when you are gone.

WARNING

This book is intended as an academic study of how criminals break the law by making false identification documents. There are experiments in this book where step-by-step instructions are given to show exactly how this is done. Some of the experiments show how government documents are forged. The creation or possession of such a document is illegal. Furthermore, the possession of any tool to make such a document is also illegal.

It is my belief that a novelty ID is legal if you place on its back a sticker containing one of the following phrases:

- Not a government document
- Novelty ID only

This is only my opinion, and I'm not a lawyer. It is your responsibility to research the laws in the state and municipality you live in and to comply with them. If you have any doubts, consult a lawyer.

Even if my opinion is correct, a law may be passed after this book is printed that makes it illegal to even think about making an ID—novelty or not. Therefore, I must advise you to seek legal counsel before thinking about creating any ID—real or fake. The penalties for ignoring this warning are very severe, and include hefty fines and lengthy imprisonment. *Thought crime* penalties imposed as such laws are passed may be even more severe.

Big Brother is watching you!

ADDITIONAL WARNING TO ANYBODY READING THIS AFTER THE YEAR 2100

It is the author's firm belief that this book will be illegal by the year 2100. If you are reading this after the year 2100, you should take it to the nearest book-burning center and ask the clerk there if it is okay for you to read it. We do not offer refunds for any book that is confiscated or burned by the government. Sorry, no exceptions.

ATTENTION MINORS (CITIZENS UNDER 21 YEARS OF AGE)

The ID examples shown in this book will not enable you to purchase alcoholic beverages.

DEFINITIONS

There are certain terms used in this book best defined in advance to ensure that we are both speaking the same language. For clarity I have defined them here.

composite photo ID: You get this type of ID when a registry clerk inserts an information card you've filled out into a special camera and takes your picture. After your waiting a few minutes, the clerk hands you a license with your picture and information all on the same laminated card. As you'll see later, there's a way to make composite photo ID without a special camera.

ID card: The actual card, paper, or film that contains identifying information, before it is laminated.

lamina: A single layer of lamination.

target state: The state whose ID you are trying to copy.

template: When used in a computer context, the template is a JPEG or PhotoShop image of a driver's license or other ID. A template is also a hand-drafted or computer-generated ID card that serves as the base document in a composite photo ID. The base document is overlaid with a head shot and security transparency, and all three layers are "shot down" into a single ID card.

vital statistics: Vital stats are the bits of information, such as weight, eye color, and birth date entered onto an ID card.

YOU: The word "you" when used in this book means you in general, not you the person reading this book. At no time should you (yes, this time I mean you) take the word "you," when used in a sentence describing illegal activity, to mean you as in you the person reading this right now (yes, I still mean you, but later on I won't mean you. Okay?). I'll just mean you in general—humans—whatever. The point is I'm not telling you (yes, you) to do anything illegal, but sentences just sound so much better when writers can liberally use the word "you" without fear that someday a law will be passed banning its use if it is used to tell you (you) to do something that Big Brother doesn't like you (I mean you) to do. Okay, so from this point forward, beginning with the next sentence, that is, "you" just means you in general and not you, you. You got that, you?

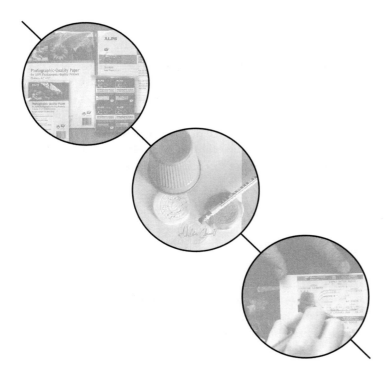

Introduction

Got ID? No? Then you can forget about cashing checks, renting cars, staying at hotels, picking up certified mail, renting a P.O. box or mail drop, getting a fishing license, obtaining a professional license, going to school, getting married, securing a loan, procuring credit, buying a home, insuring yourself or your property, purchasing a gun, renting videos, getting a job, or starting a business . . . among other things.

So what? Most people have ID, right? Right. Sure, plop down your ID to rent a car and then check your mailbox the following week. You'll find ads from every car rental agent in your area, applications for auto loans, and requests for charitable contributions, among other uninvited intrusions into your personal affairs and habits.

Then try to sit down and eat your dinner. You'll note a distinctive ringing sound coming from a certain white box hanging on your wall. Answer it. Guess who? It's the IRS telling you your lifestyle exceeds your income. You're being audited. It seems a gas station attendant should not be able to afford the frivolity of renting a car.

Past debts? Use your ID to open a P.O. box and then go home and wait for the bill collectors to call. Then try to sleep. You'll note a distinctive rapping on the large, wooden, rectangular panel securing egress to your front walkway. You open the door. Guess what? It's the sheriff's department. Who's standing behind the sheriff? A representative of U.O. Repo Depot asking for your car keys.

But you're a stand-up citizen? Good. You can rest in the comfort of knowing your state-issued ID entitles you to the automatic entry of your name and personal information in more than 10,000 government and corporate databases. You'll feel secure knowing that if you ever step out of line, the feds will find you faster than you can say "D.B. Cooper," and you'll have the privilege of paying your debt to society all the sooner.

So what can you do? Nothing. Some people use fake IDs, but unfortunately they are illegal, so there's not a goddamned thing you can do about the fact that you are merely a number in the system's supercomputers—subject to its whims, errors, and omissions for the rest of your pushed, filed, stamped, indexed, briefed, debriefed, and numbered existence.

But since there is a nasty element out there whose members, despite the good law, continue to manufacture and use fake IDs, I have decided to write a book about how those good-for-nothing, anti-social, just-hafta-go-their-own-way, subversive bastards go about it—just in case you'd like to know for your own information.

WHAT THIS BOOK WILL DO FOR YOU

This book will teach you how subversive bastards make identification cards. You will learn about the following:

- Printers, scanners, cameras, software, and other equipment crooks used to make fake IDs
- How pugnacious punks use the latest equipment as well as the old standbys
- Groundbreaking research in hologram reproduction and how hoodwinking hoodlums use this information when constructing fake IDs
- How unchivalrous sharks make IDs from computer templates
- How filthy-fingered filchers create composite IDs with a standard 35mm camera
- Various ways bellicose bandits fake notary, corporate, city, and state seals
- Where criminals get away with cutting corners and where they don't

Some naughty people have ID dreams deeper than their pockets. Therefore, I will share with you many "poor man's" techniques that such nasties use to make professional-looking IDs. Some licentious lechers decide that making IDs is too much work. I'll show you where they buy IDs so you can make sure to stay the hell away from such evil places.

WHO IN HELL AM I, AND WHAT DO I KNOW ABOUT MAKING ID?

I am the state's worst nightmare: a licensed private detective who is also a staunch privacy advocate and freedom fighter. While private detectives are typically thought of as privacy invaders as opposed to preservers, most of my cases are aimed at the system. I won my detective license after suing the system for trying to keep it from me.

Over the years I've investigated corrupt cops, dirty politicians, overzealous condo board presidents, and a host of other creeps who deserved what they got. What better way to maintain privacy than by exposing the private lives of politicians who introduce privacy-restricting bills into the legislature?

But it takes a long time to fight the system, and I don't expect to see a truly private world in my lifetime. Many of my clients have felt the same. Even though the feds like to think of ID forgers as lowlife subversive scum, there are privacy seekers in the world who have found good uses for fake IDs. It has become necessary for privacy seekers to create new identities to shield themselves from the barrage of intrusive bureaucracies and their endless need to know every facet of our existence.

One aspect of maintaining such identities is the use of novelty identification, also known as "fake ID." If you've read my book *The Modern Identity Changer,* then you know I've helped many people disappear over the years. Although most of my clients end up with new state-issued documents, they've had to conquer a great many hurdles along the way to getting them. Usually, conquering such hurdles is facilitated by the use of false identification. Since it's dangerous for a disappearing client to use the services of a back-alley ID man, oftentimes I had to make IDs for my clients.

I still have the first ID I every made for a client. It sucked. It was an employment ID that my client used to open a bank account in his new name. Even though the ID was laughable—even I still get a good chuckle today when I look at it—the bank rep simply said, "I'll have to make a copy of this." Then she opened the account. Purpose served.

Then came the desktop computer revolution. An apparent boon for document forgers, but in truth, and as you will see, it was the worst thing that could have happened for privacy seekers. But, lo, I was just one man, and one man cannot stanch the rush of progressing technology. I had to ride the dragon. Reluctantly, I learned about computers. I learned programming: BASIC, C, then C++, and now HTML and JavaScript. I learned graphical user interfaces (GUIs) and object-oriented programming, learned to master computer-aided design (CAD) programs, word processors, and graphics software. I was faithful and stayed on top of all the bugs and reengineering, all the mergers and takeovers, even as I screamed inside knowing all along what would happen.

And it happened.

It's happening now. Too many people are using desktop computer technology to make IDs and even to counterfeit money. Now the feds are making IDs harder than ever to reproduce, and, as you may have noticed, the almighty buck is being redesigned to thwart modern desktop counterfeiters. The system is introducing counterfeit-resistant security devices—ones that are not readily replicated by commercial desktop computers and accessories. Holograms and magnetic swipe cards are two examples. As you'll learn, there are still ways to make holograms and magnetic swipes, but I fear for the future. This may be the last book ever to show how state identification cards can be economically reproduced.

Even though the very first ID I ever made was completely awful, I'm thankful that I've refined my technique over the years. Today I am very proud of the IDs I make: they are rarely questioned.

I tell you this only so you'll understand where my knowledge came from. I do not intend to promote the use of fake ID in this book, whether for privacy protection purposes or otherwise. I've already written two books promoting the use of fake ID for privacy purposes, and I do not intend to write any more about this subject. Why? Because times are changing, folks. I fully believe we are moving into an era of book banning. There are already books in this country that are effectively banned because some bad court decisions have left publishers open to crushing lawsuits. Frankly, I don't want to have to rewrite this book after our brain-dead reps in Congress decide to go the way of Australia and other countries that literally maintain lists of banned books. That's why this book is written as an exposé of a certain criminal element in our degraded society. As such, it should be one of the last to be banned. If you have concerns about book banning, please make your congressional representative aware of them. It is unlikely that your rep will have original concerns of his or her own: such requires actual thought.

Now that you know who I am, how I got to know what I know, and what I'm going to teach you, let's talk about who you are, who you shouldn't be, and what you better not learn.

WHO ARE YOU, AND WHAT'RE 'YA TRYIN' TO PULL?

If you are a minor thinking about using the methods in this book to purchase alcoholic beverages, think again. First of all, let me just remind you that this book is for *academic study only!* Using the techniques discussed here to pull a fast one on the state will get you in deep shit. When you get caught (and you will), you may lose your driving privileges. You will probably give up any shot at getting into a decent college; you will never become an attorney, a doctor, or a professional deserving public trust. You will destroy any political aspirations you may have because the press will look up your conviction (and you will be convicted) and tell the whole world about it. Besides, alcohol will RUIN YOUR LIFE. Take it from one who knows. If I hadn't spent 16 years at the bottom of a shot glass, I'd be a millionaire by now. Alcohol saps your motivation, drains your ambition, and makes you hate the world—not to mention the devastating physical consequences, which, by the way, are IRREVERSIBLE. To wit: liver damage and loss of brain cells—both, I'll repeat, IRREVERSIBLE! You will gain a better, more powerful perspective on life if you hang back and drink soda water at the parties you attend. Watch how all the drunks make fools of themselves. You will eventually notice someone of the opposite sex—or same sex if that is your preference—who is also drinking soda water. My advice: hang with that person. Go to movies, walk along the beach, take long drives in the country, or curl up on the couch with nachos and a video. You will find these things infinitely more rewarding than sitting around pouring poison into your gut and talking in incomplete clichés until you puke. Okay? Enough said.

ADDITIONAL NOTE TO MINORS

Just in case the foregoing meant nothing to you, I must give you fair warning. Since this is a book for *informational purposes only*, the driver's license templates I've chosen are the most commonly forged documents in the United States. Therefore, they are completely useless for alcohol-related purposes. For example, there are so many fake New Jersey IDs out there that many liquor store owners and bar bouncers no longer accept the legitimate New Jersey license as proof of age. The few who do accept them have become experts at detecting fakes. In short, any attempt to use the template-based IDs in this book for illicit purposes will *more than likely* get you caught. If you think I'm just saying this to cover my ass, check out what the Internet has to say about the New Jersey and other popular IDs. They are useless for purchasing alcohol.

HOW TO USE THIS BOOK

You can't. Using this book is illegal. If you have a problem with this, speak to your congressional representative and then hold your breath. You may study the pictures, learn how good-for-nothing bastards make IDs in the back alleys of good ol' U.S. of A., and maybe—just maybe—make one or two "novelty" IDs yourself, which at least at the moment, I don't think would be too illegal. But don't quote me on that. The laws are subject to change at the whims of rich people, who, for the most part, are born into their roles and have little idea of the impact of their legislation, much less the intellect to comprehend the hell that will result from it.

BUT AREN'T THERE LEGITIMATE USES FOR FAKE ID?

Aren't you listening? It doesn't matter. The government has spoken. Fake ID of any kind is *mala prohibita.* It's a no-no 'cuz our government says so. It doesn't matter how you plan to use it. It doesn't matter what horrible situation you need to escape from. Nor does the government give a shit about any unalienable rights you think you were born with. That's all out the window now that we have gone the way George Orwell told us in *1984.*

But My State DMV Sold My Current Address to My Ex-Husband, Who Has Repeatedly Threatened to Kill Me and My Children!

That's not an excuse to use fake ID. Under the current law, you have to allow your ex-husband to kill you and your children. What's a few dead kids compared to the sacred laws that are the pillars of our great society? How can you even begin to compare children—who are usually under 4 feet tall—to the great pillars, typically imagined by patriots to be well over 200 feet tall? That's *at least* a 196-foot difference. What's wrong with you?

But My Credit Profile Has Been Crossed with a Deadbeat's Whose Name Is Similar to Mine!

Haven't you heard about the pillars? Our government defends us from nuclear attack, biological devastation, threats of insurrection, attempted coups, serial killers, rapists, and people who live on ranches. Recently our government has even taken the magnanimous step to protect us from books with improper information—stuff no good citizen should ever see. How can you be so shallow as to care about your credit rating? The pillars must be protected. Measly credit mishaps are no excuse for using fake ID.

But I Inherited a Vicious Criminal Record Due to an National Crime Information Center Computer Glitch, and the Government Doesn't Believe Me!

The government doesn't believe you because you are lying. If you were telling the truth, your statement would not contradict the omniscient government database. At any rate, it's still not an excuse to use fake ID. Under the current law, you must allow the government to prosecute you for murder; then you must participate in the state's capital punishment program. But fear not. Your murder is sanctioned by the state. If you have a choice, go with cyanide gas. Some interesting things happen to your lungs, muscles, and bones when you inhale cyanide. Make your last experience an intense one.

But What about Camouflage Passports? Why Does the Government Allow Them? Isn't That a Contradiction? *WTF*?

Camouflage passports are typically used by inner party delegates traveling to Third World countries. We must protect the party members at all costs. They know what's best for us. How would we survive if something happened to them? For these reasons, the government tolerates camouflage passport use by the proletariat. Yes, it contradicts the False Identification Crime Control Act, but just doublethink it. You'll be okay. Big Brother will lead you.

NOW THAT YOU KNOW THE RULES . . .

If you make an ID that contains false or misleading information about precisely who in hell you are, it is probably illegal to take it anywhere beyond your living room. It is definitely illegal to show it to anybody in an effort to convince that person that you are someone or some age that you, in fact, are not. Even if your name, address, age, and other vital stats appear correctly on the ID, it is still illegal if it purports to be issued by any governing body or if it contains a Social Security number—or other mark of the beast—that is not your true state-issued serial number. If you break the law, you will go to jail for many years, where you will most likely be raped by inmates and beaten by the guards. The tricks you are about to learn are performed in this book without mirrors. I do not use safety nets, and many of these procedures are performed high above the circus floor at dangerous speeds. In short: *do not try this at home.*

Section One

METHODOLOGY, TOOLS, AND MATERIALS

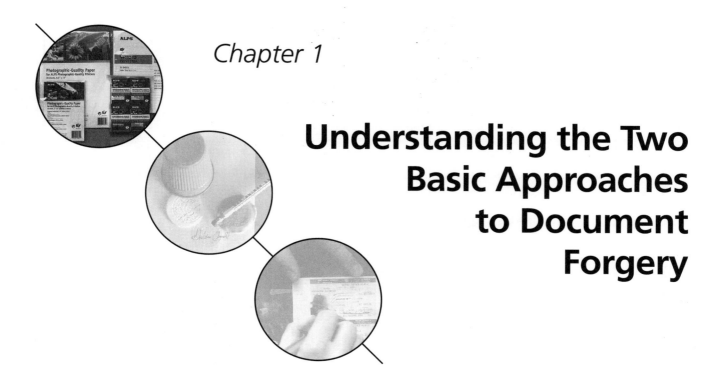

Chapter 1

Understanding the Two Basic Approaches to Document Forgery

There are two basic approaches that hooligans use to make fake IDs. I'll introduce both here so that you can get a taste of each. You might decide that an academic study of both techniques quenches your curiosity. Conversely, you may become partial to one or the other of them, and decide to focus your learning. Either way, their explanation will aid your understanding of upcoming chapters and the general layout of this book.

THE NEW SCHOOL (USING MODERN TECHNOLOGY)

The feds are learning that malcontents and sociopathic monsters use home computers to commit the horrendous crime of counterfeiting identity documents. The home computer process involves making or obtaining a digital copy or *template* of a real ID, such as a driver's license. The hoodlum then uses his personal computer to alter the template. This usually involves digitally pasting a recent self-portrait onto the template, accompanied by appropriate identifying information and whatever name, birth date, and Social Security number he desires.

The self-portrait is scanned into the computer or downloaded from a digital camera. All template editing is done by sophisticated graphics software, which neatly handles bleeds, screens, and overlapping text often used to secure the ID. The end result is sent to a high-resolution desktop color printer.

Special security devices known as holograms can also be printed with a desktop printer. The hologram can be printed directly onto the template, onto a special transparency sheet, or directly onto the laminated ID.

THE OLD SCHOOL

Psychopaths and mental defectives of the old school make fake IDs using basic art skills and old-fashioned (nondigital) photography. They steal templates or make them from scratch and then use an appropriate typewriter to enter whatever information they'd like. They use an actual passport photograph and create overlaps with transparency sheets.

Once the template is ready, it is then "shot down" with a 35mm camera to create a one-piece ID card. For some applications, "old-school" results can be superior to modern technology.

AND WHERE THE TWAIN SHALL MEET

There are certain things common to both methods. Once a template is printed—either by computer or at the local pharmacy—crooks need to trim it, add a backing, add a hologram, and laminate.

There are other times when naughty people commingle modern technology with old-school methods. Let's say a certain felon has plenty of photography equipment but no artistic skill. Well, rather than draw a template, he might wish to design one using the local library's computer. Voilà! New school meets old. For desperate criminals it's whatever works.

Now let's examine some ID-making tools and materials, new school and old.

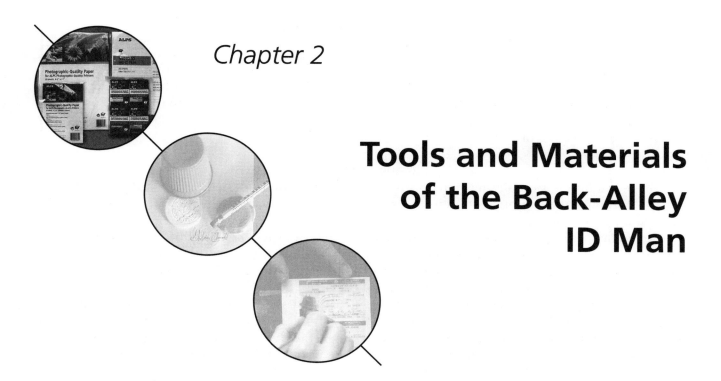

Chapter 2

Tools and Materials of the Back-Alley ID Man

This chapter introduces the tools and materials I used to make the IDs described and depicted in this book. I briefly describe why a particular tool was chosen and show where bad people purchase such egregious contraband. Details of how depraved degenerates use each tool will come later.

It is by no means required that all these tools be purchased to make IDs. The casual reader can make an academic study of ID forgery with a minimal cash outlay. In fact, you may already own everything needed to perform some modest experiments in this art.

Nor is it required that the exact tools I use be purchased. You may already own or have access to substantially equivalent tools and materials to get the job done. With some minor alterations to the procedures presented later, you should be able to use substitutes with a minimum of fuss. After all, "take a picture" means the same thing whether you're using an old Sears KS-1 like yours truly or a top-of-the line 10-megapixel digital camera; *laminate* means the same thing whether you're using Kinko's or some peel-and-stick lamination sheets from a Cracker Jack box; *print* means print. You get the idea.

A WORD ABOUT RESOLUTION

Much of what follows requires an understanding of the term *resolution* as it relates to computer monitors, printers, scanners, and digital cameras. If you know this stuff inside out, feel free to skip ahead. If you've always been confused by the term, this section should help.

Printer manufacturers are always talking about resolution. But what is it? What resolution is high enough to print IDs? Those are good questions and ones often asked. If you're going to buy equipment to make novelty IDs, you'll need to know the answers. Not only will you need to know about printer resolution, you'll also need to know how to set the resolution of your computer monitor, determine the maximum resolution of your digital camera, and calculate the final resolution of the ID templates you edit. If you don't know what an ID template is, don't worry. We'll get to that too. For now, let's get a firm handle on resolution.

There are two types of resolution: image and color.

Image Resolution

Image resolution is usually given in dots per inch (dpi). Printers—whether laser, inkjet, or Micro Dry™— form images with tiny dots of ink or toner. The more dots a printer can squeeze into an inch, the more detailed the image will be.

Generally speaking, a high-resolution image is one that can trick the brain into thinking it sees a complete picture rather than a series of dots. Since we are ultimately concerned with printing a believable picture (i.e., an ID card), let's explore exactly what that means. This book's old-school ID methods use standard photography to accomplish this. Let's begin there.

Photography, literally, means "drawing with light." We, of course, know that we are not making an exact clone of the object we are photographing—that technology is only available in bad science-fiction movies. Rather, we are sampling the light reflected by the object and recording it on film.

Just as an artist looks at his subject and paints a white dot to indicate a highlight, a camera—analog or digital—records what it "sees" as dots of color.

In reality, our eyes see in dots of color. Speaking loosely, the "resolution" of our eyes is billions of "dots" per square inch. There is no technology that can match the human eye—not even our best color print films. But where the eyes can't be fooled, the brain can. The human brain is fairly gullible. With enough convincing, we can get the brain to believe it sees something it really doesn't.

Two good examples are summertime "puddle" mirages and the large, looming harvest moon we see—or, rather, *think* we see—at the beginning of every fall.

In the summertime, direct sunlight heats the asphalt streets to temperatures that most bare feet can't tolerate. The air just above the street also becomes heated as evidenced by those waves of heat we sometimes see coming off the road. But the air several inches above the road is much cooler. This difference in temperature causes light from just above the horizon to refract, or bend, back up and away from the pavement. Looking down a long road toward the horizon, our eyes see the blue sky sitting on the road. But the brain doesn't believe it. The brain is not used to seeing the sky on the road. The brain is used to seeing puddles on the road and does us the favor of making a minor adjustment to the image so that it fits better with the world we've come to know. Neat, huh?

So what about that moon? Around the autumnal (and, for that matter, the vernal) equinox, the moon follows a much shallower path along the horizon. It does not get up as high as it does in summer and winter. Therefore, when the moon rises during these times, it travels just above familiar foreground objects, such as tree lines and rooftops. Because these familiar objects are generally large, our brain tells us that the moon is also large. Don't believe it? Next time you *think* you see this "large" moon, perform this simple experiment. Turn around so that the moon is at your back. Then, bend over and look at it upside down from between your legs. Because the once familiar foreground objects are now upside down and no longer familiar, the moon—for a moment—will look the same size it always does when it is high in the sky. Try it. It works!

Knowing what we now know about our gullible brain, we can see where a photograph only needs to have enough dots of information to fool our brain into thinking it's seeing something complete, when, in fact, it is not. Now this is where it begins to get complicated. A newspaper photograph is a good place to begin understanding this concept. Look at one. Look at it from across the room and then look at it closely under a bright light. Now look at it real close under a magnifying glass.

You'll note that from across the room the photograph looks pretty realistic. When it's under a bright light you begin to get an idea where certain details of the photo are lacking, and under a magnifying glass you will clearly see that the picture is made up of many tiny dots.

A color photograph, such as a snapshot from your recent vacation, is more convincing to the eye. This is because a standard 35mm color negative contains about 6 million "dots" of information, whereas the same size newspaper photo only has a few thousand.

The trend in computer periphery is to produce "photo-quality" images and printouts. But what does that mean? A magazine generally prints its photos at about 200 dpi, and they are considered photo quality. I'll tell you right now, 200 dpi is definitely not good enough for novelty IDs. One can be thankful that, even very inexpensive printers today produce at least 600-dpi printouts, which is the bare minimum for believable IDs.[1]

Color Resolution

Color resolution is the number of separate colors your printer, monitor, or other device can display at the same time. Early printers and monitors were monochrome, which literally means "one color." Later devices, such as enhanced graphics adaptor (EGA) monitors and color ribbon printers, were capable of only a few colors.

Today, color resolution is discussed in "bits" of color data. Eight-bit color resolution means your monitor is capable of producing 256 separate colors at once. This is because computer data are binary and each bit of information can either be "on" or "off," leaving a total of two possibilities. Two (possibilities) raised to the eighth (number of bits) power equals 256. Sixteen-bit color is 2^{16}—totaling 65,536 colors.

All you'll ever really need is 24- or 30-bit color resolution. Anything more than that is just a marketing ploy. Just remember that $2^{24} = 16.7$ million colors, which is about as many as the human eye can distinguish. For this reason, 24-bit color is known as "true color," a term you may have heard in reference to scanners, printers, and monitors.

It is good that most computer devices manufactured today are true color. When buying a printer, scanner, or digital camera, make sure that it's marketed as 24-bit, true-color, or 16.7-million-color device. It's less important to have a true-color monitor, but you will need at least 8-bit (256) color resolution to accurately edit ID templates and to use most of the software we'll be discussing.

Setting Your Monitor's Resolution

You will need to check your system setup to make sure it is set for at least 256 colors and 800 x 600 screen resolution. On a personal computer running Windows 95, click Start, Settings, Control Panel, Display, Settings. If you've purchased your computer recently, you should find that everything is in order or can easily be changed. If the proper options are not available, you will need to select Change Display Type. If other device drivers are not available, you may need to upgrade your monitor. Contact your monitor's manufacturer for more information. For preliminary ID work, you may be able to get by with 16 colors and 640 x 480 display. As you upgrade to more sophisticated software, expect the installation program to complain about your display setup.

Calculating the Image Resolution of Your Final Printout

Even an Alps Micro Dry (MD) 5000 printer, which prints 2,400 dpi, does you little good if your original image is only 100 dpi. There are several things you must consider. First, what is the resolution of the original ID template? If you scanned the template yourself with a 600-dpi scanner, your final image will never be more than 600 dpi. If you want the full use of your 2,400-dpi printer, you will need a scanner that scans at 2,400 dpi, or you'll need to find ID templates on the Internet that are at least 2,400 dpi.[2]

Digital camera technology adds a layer of difficulty in calculating the dpi of your final printout. This is because digital cameras are marketed according to total dots rather than dots per inch. (When discussing digital cameras, we use the term *pixels* instead of dots, but for our purposes the terms are interchangeable.)

To determine a digital photo's resolution, you need to know the target size of your finished product. You then divide the target width, measured in inches, by the pixel width of the camera's digital sensor, or CCD. The result is the dpi of the final printout (assuming the printer's resolution is sufficient).

Here is the formula:

$$CCD_W/T_W = dpi$$

Where CCD_W is the pixel width of the camera's digital sensor and T_W is the target's width in inches.

For example, let's say I photograph my kitty cat with my D-340R digital camera. This camera has a 1,280 x 960 CCD. Let's further assume that the picture is perfect and needs no cropping. Therefore, I'd like to print it in its entirety for use in a 12 x 9-inch picture frame. My CCD_W, then, is 1,280, and my target width is 12. Calculated out we have 1,280/12 = 106.67 dpi. This is probably sufficient to put kitty's picture on the fridge but is not acceptable for novelty IDs. Fortunately, novelty IDs are much smaller, which will yield a much higher resolution.

The astute observer will have noted the calculation for height also yields the same result: 960/9 = 106.67 dpi. In practice, there will be times when your target's dimensions do not have the same ratio as your camera's CCD, in this case 4/3. When that happens, you will usually have to crop the image so it fits the dimensions of your target. Provided you do not change the aspect ratio when resizing your digital images (and you shouldn't), the dpi will be the same for height as it is for width.

Moving On

This section has introduced you to resolution and how it affects the quality of novelty IDs. This information will help you make informed decisions when shopping for and using the tools of this trade, assuming you choose to make an academic study of ID forgery. Now let's have a look at some of my favorite ID-making tools.

FIRST THE BIG STUFF

In choosing tools for this book—at least as far as the expensive stuff was concerned—I had to somewhat revamp and update my ID construction methods. I wanted to show the tools most often used by degenerate slimeball counterfeiters, but I also wanted to keep costs down. I'm happy to report that my compromises were not so gut retching. Here are some tools that will do a good job on your novelty IDs, but not on your wallet.

Adobe PhotoShop

It wouldn't be fair to go into lengthy explanations of PhotoShop 6.0: purchasing this software would be cost-prohibitive for most readers. At the time of this writing it was selling for around $700— ouch! A computer system capable of running the software could easily have doubled that figure and then some.

Luckily, the two most important PhotoShop features are available in earlier versions of the software. PhotoShop 3.0 allows you to render graphics in multiple layers; that's the first important feature. Second, you can adjust the opacity of each layer, which comes in handy for making holograms and watermarks. These features are extremely useful to the ID artisan, as you will see in coming

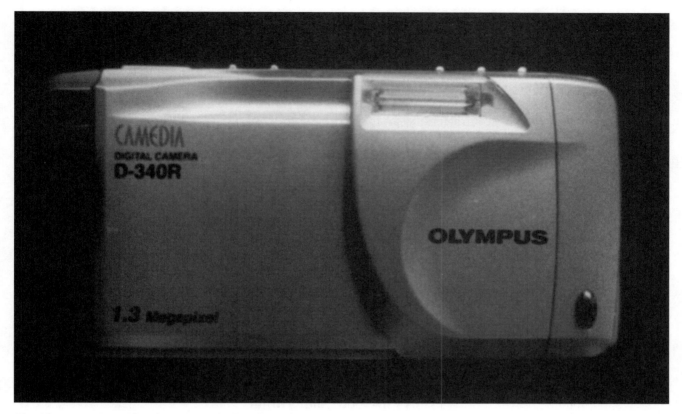

The Olympus D-340R digital camera is the best bang for the buck.

chapters. PhotoShop 3.0 offers a myriad of sophisticated graphic-rendering features in addition to the nifty ones above.

I was able to purchase a "used" version of PhotoShop 3.0 on eBay[3] for $85. Of course, there are those very few document forgers who are also unscrupulous enough to buy bootleg or "backup" versions of this (and other) software for around $10 (perish the thought!). Then there are those who can easily afford PhotoShop 6.0. If you are one of these folks, either unscrupulous or rich, then by all means enjoy the more sophisticated version of this wonderfully useful software—if it will run on your computer. Just be advised that the commands referenced in this book are for PhotoShop 3.0.

Olympus D-340R Digital Camera

To make believable IDs, subversive bastards need high-resolution photos of themselves. It ain't gonna matter a whit if your printer has 2,400-dpi resolution if your original image is only 72 dpi.

Generally speaking, you'll need at least a "megapixel" camera to get consistently professional results. The D-340R has a resolution of 1,280 x 960 (1.3 megapixels). I think it's the best digital camera in its price range. By the time this goes to print, you might be able to find a used one on the market for around $100. Mine cost $300 new in 1999.

The D-340R has two useful functions. First, it's great for taking various self-portraits against different backgrounds. Many novice identity changers make the mistake of using the same picture on every ID. If arrested, the cop impounding the novice's wallet will notice this immediately, thereby ruining any chance of the novice passing himself off as somebody else. The traditional solution was to have several passport photos taken in different clothing and hairstyles. Though this is still an option, digital self-portraits offer greater flexibility. What if you need a backdrop color other than blue? This may indeed be required for matching various state, university, and corporate ID cards. In the past, ID forgers had to bring their own backdrop to the camera studio (which might arouse suspicion) or do their own photography at home and hope for a good picture. Both are costly and time-consuming processes.

Since most ID photos are just a few square centimeters in size, a printed image taken with a D-340R (or comparable camera) easily meets our minimum 600-dpi standard (see under "A Word about Resolution" above). Today, counterfeiters can make their own ID photos quickly and effectively at home. By doing so, they eliminate exposure (no pun intended) to passport photographers and film developers, who may become suspicious and alert authorities to the odd behavior they witness. What odd behavior? A person who for no good reason brings a backdrop to the passport photo studio; an unphotogenic schmuck who sends in three film rolls of self-portraits; a shaggy dude who shows up wearing his "Counterfeiters Do It on Printing Presses" T-shirt. Okay, I exaggerate. Chances are the film police don't care about any of this; they just want your money. But if you should be caught for something (God knows what) after the fact, you don't want any unusual behavior left fresh in the minds of clerks who are otherwise desperately bored and would love to impress the authorities with their astute observation abilities.

The D-340R can also be used in a pinch to make ID templates. You can photograph a 2 3/4 x 1 3/4-inch state license yielding a 465-dpi printout, which may be good enough for some circumstances. Good-for-nothing son-of-a-bitch document forgers do this by placing the camera on a tripod 4 inches above a real ID and snapping a picture in macro mode. Using the wide-angle lens at this close range will produce a distorted image. The ID's sides, especially the long side, will appear bowed out. The sons-o'-bitches solve this problem by putting the ID in a vise and closing it slightly so the ID surface becomes concave (the middle bends down). This compensates for the distortion produced by the camera.

Alps MD-5000 Color Printer

If you've been reading closely, you've probably guessed that I'm in love with the Alps MD-5000. Technology is progressing fast, and 10 years from now I'll probably look back on my love affair with the Alps as a mere infatuation. But in today's market there is no comparable printer in its price range.

If you shop around, you can get the printer and dye-sublimation upgrade for under $500 brand new. At the time of this writing, factory-reconditioned models were available for around $300 with full warranty. I got mine from buy.com. The printer was $418, and the upgrade kit was $71. Shortly after I bought it, I saw the printer for $404 from some store in New Jersey (can't remember which).

The printer and upgrade come with all necessary cartridges. But while you're shopping, pick up the EconoBlack and Gold Metallic cartridges. The EconoBlack will save unnecessary use of your other cartridges when printing business letters; the Gold Metallic comes in handy for certain types of holograms. You'll also want to throw the following into your shopping cart before checkout:

- Vphoto print film, item #105829
- Photographic-quality paper, item #105824 (4 x 6) or #105822 (8 1/2 x 11)
- Photographic-quality labels, item #105848 (3 x 2)

I must warn you up front that the paper is not cheap. At this writing, 20 sheets of photographic paper costs about $13 at buy.com. Vphoto print film sells at about $6 for 20 sheets. Fortunately, you only need the paper for your final drafts. I do my regular drafts with HammerMill Laser Print Radiant White (basis 24/60) paper, UPC #010199004604. Visit the Web site at www.hammermillpapers.com for more information. Most common laser printer papers should work fine with the Alps.

When I get close to a finished draft, I use the Alps Vphoto primer cartridge, which comes with the printer and allows you to use regular laser printer paper in Vphoto mode. To reduce expensive mistakes, I insert Vphoto print film or photographic paper only when I'm all done tweaking the template.

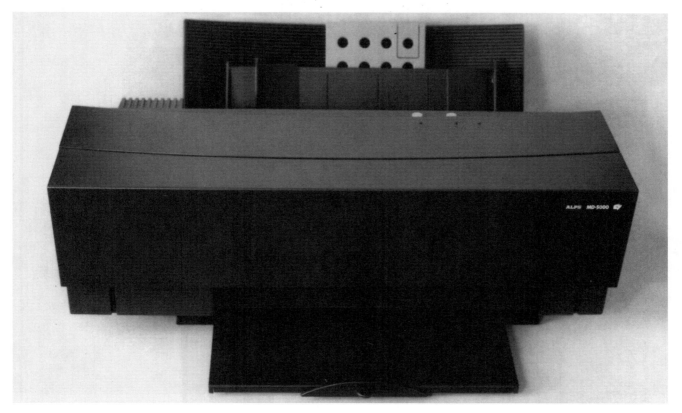

Here she comes, Miss Ameri . . . Ahem. Yes, I still overreact when it comes to this impeccably engineered beauty, the Alps MD-5000 printer. Get one while they last.

You can also save money by printing several ID templates on one sheet. I wait until I have several final drafts ready, and then I insert them as picture objects into a word processor and print them all onto one 8 1/2 x 11 sheet of photo paper. But I'm getting ahead of myself. You're probably not going to purchase a damn thing until I share with you the virtues of this printer. So here goes.

Alps has developed and patented a completely different way of desktop printing, which is called the Micro Dry, or MD, method. As its name implies, the ink goes on the paper dry. This prevents unwanted absorption of ink by the paper, which is a common problem with inkjet printers. Because of the ink absorption phenomenon, an inkjet printer dot grows a fuzzy sort of halo around it immediately after it is printed, and this severely affects the overall quality of inkjet printouts.

The MD process dot has no halo around it. Alps takes full advantage of this fact by giving its printers the ability to print dots of varying sizes. With the ink absorption problem out of the way, it is much easier for the printer to control the dot size. This allows the Alps to print in finer detail, especially at curves, corners, and edges.

A 2,400-dpi image printed on Vphoto print film rivals 35mm color prints. In fact, if you can get 2,400-dpi templates, you may wish to forgo purchasing the dye-sublimation upgrade kit. But as mentioned earlier, true 2,400-dpi images are hard to find and even harder to work with. That's why I'm also a fan of Alps' dye-sublimation upgrade kit.

F*^@#^#*@#*ck!!! (Alps Update)

During the later stages of writing this book, a reader brought to my attention a very disturbing update regarding Alps Electric Co., Ltd. Without any warning or given reason, Alps decided to stop

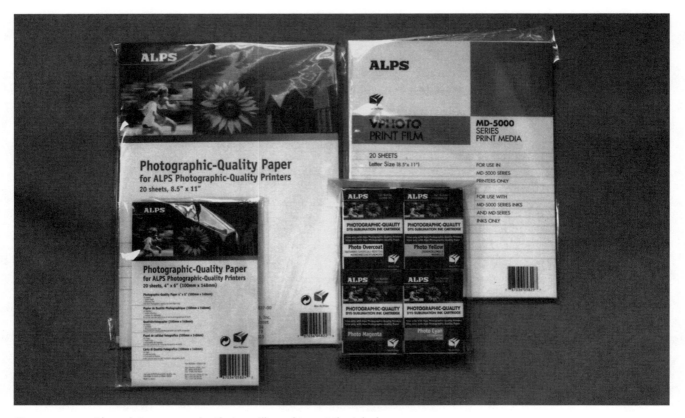

Here are some Alps printer accessories that you'll need to get the job done.

manufacturing its line of MD printers. I contacted a service rep from buyalps.com who explained that the MD technology had been sold to another company, but even the rep did not know what the other company was. It is unclear at this time whether MD technology will be available in the future.

At the time of this update, there were several Alps printers for sale on eBay, but I was unable to find any store that stocks them. The new Alps 5000s on eBay were bid up as high as $795 due to the shortage, but I think they are worth even that inflated price.

Okay, So What's the Deal with Dye-Sub?

Dye-sublimation is a thermal process where ink is embedded into the matrix of a special paper. A medium-resolution image, say 280 dpi, will look like a photograph when printed with this unique process. ID thugs like dye-sublimation because it produces very realistic IDs even when the original template is not of the highest possible resolution.

Color Scanner

Although it's true that scanners are dropping in price, I'm not so sure the inexpensive ones are exactly high resolution. Most "discount" models that claim to be 600 dpi, really have 300-dpi scanning elements. So how do retailers get away with advertising these imposters as 600 dpi? As always, a cautious consumer must read the fine print. Chances are, upon closer inspection of the box, you'll discover embedded among the eye-reddening fine print a new term, *interpolation*.

Interpolation means that the 300-dpi scanning element uses software or firmware to guess what the other 300 pixels might be. This is no different than attempting to change a 300-dpi image into a

600-dpi image by saving it as a different size file in a graphics program such as Adobe PhotoShop. This trick may indeed produce 600 dpi, but the "resolution" is still 300 dpi.

So you should always check the specs when shopping for a scanner. To compare apples to apples, you will need to know the resolution of the scanning element, not the interpolated dpi. The resolution is shown as *optical resolution* on the box. If the box says 1,200 x 600 dpi but does not specify optical resolution, be wary.

At the same time, do not run away just because a box uses the word *interpolation*. It is quite possible that a scanner will have 600 x 1,200-dpi optical resolution and 4,800 x 9,600-interpolated dpi. That's fine. The interpolation routine can be thought of as an extra in this case.

There are plenty of good scanners out there, and they all pretty much work on the same principle. Therefore, I see no need to recommend a specific unit for this book. In fact, if you own a digital camera, you can get through many of the experiments in this book without a scanner (see under "Olympus D-340R Digital Camera" on page 15).

Word Processor

I put this under "First the Big Stuff" because good word processing software can cost you a handsome nickel. If at all possible, purchase or otherwise obtain Office 97 Pro. Office 2000 is of course available if you prefer and if it will run on your machine. Either package contains Microsoft Word, which I am using right now as I type. Many swindlers use MS Word to make employment and student ID templates. These bad guys also use Word to make ID backs, rather than counting on the fuzzy or nonexistent scans found (or not found) on the Internet. Although PhotoShop's "Type" feature makes nice ID backs, the resulting file uses much more memory than a Word file does.

If you're lucky, your computer came loaded with Word as many do nowadays. If you're not lucky and can't otherwise obtain this software, don't sweat it too much. Your computer probably has a stock word processor that will help you produce ID templates and backs. These lesser quality word processors are harder to use, and you probably won't be able to make watermarks and other fun stuff, but it will get you started in the art.

TOOLS FROM THE OLD SCHOOL

Those of you who know me, either personally or through my books, are aware that I'm a big fan of old-fashioned methods and "poor man's" techniques for doing just about anything. Even if you're tied by an umbilical cord to your PC, you might still want to explore some of the more old-fashioned methods I'll be presenting. If nothing else, you will gain a greater appreciation for modern tools and how much time they can save. If you're like me, you'll see where the latest gadgets have limitations and you'll develop an affinity for some of the old standbys.

Photography

I've had a lifelong love of photography and the arts in general. So making IDs with a single lens reflex (SLR) camera was not so foreign to me when I first began doing it. If you've never used anything but an "instamatic" type of camera, the prospect of beginning a whole new hobby just to learn how creeps make IDs may seem daunting. But you need not think of it that way.

There are really just a few aspects of photography that one must learn to make novelty IDs. So if you're not interested in getting all wrapped up in a new hobby, you needn't be concerned. You can buy some fairly inexpensive equipment to get the shots you'll need. But don't be surprised if you start taking your camera along on vacations and day trips. The art of photography can be quite absorbing.

You can spend under $100 for used photography equipment to make IDs. At this writing, eBay has Sears KS-1 SLR cameras listed for $15 to $35 and macro lenses for around $15.

Those two items alone are enough photo equipment to make IDs. I suggest two more items: a Slik tripod with quick-release mount (around $12 on eBay) and a mechanical shutter release cable (between $5 and $10 on eBay). You may be able to find all of these items at a yard sale for much less.

Typewriter

In my book *Identity, Privacy & Personal Freedom: Big Brother vs. The New Resistance,* I included an extensive list of typewriters, detailing the years during which each was in widespread use. This information comes in very handy for anarchistic psychopaths who insist on forging old vital records just to get an Irish passport.[4]

Here's a short list of typewriters document forgers have been known to use:

- IBM Selectric, Selectric II—recent documents
- Remington Rem-ette—1938
- Remington No. 17—1939
- Corona—1912, produced until 1941; good for documents between 1912 and 1950
- Underwood—1901

For older records recalcitrant rogues must resort to pen and ink. An exceptionally stupid rogue might try to forge old birth and marriage records with a ballpoint pen (which wasn't invented until 1938 and not in widespread use until the 1950s). I'm sure you can imagine what fresh hell such foolhardiness would wreak.

Poor Man's Lamination

Lamination pouches are not expensive, but laminators are. Some fledgling filchers simply use several layers of peel-and-stick lamination sheets to give their IDs a thick, laminated feel.

Peel-and-stick lamination is actually the simplest form of cold lamination. Cold lamination is a simple way to avoid some of the detrimental effects of heat lamination discussed later.

STUFF YOU'LL NEED—OLD SCHOOL OR NEW

Whether you have all the latest gadgets or struggle with an old SLR camera, at some point you'll have to put all the ID pieces/parts together. You'll need to perform hands-on trimming, tweaking, gluing, and TLC. ID forgers need stencil knives, glue sticks, holographic film, tape, bond paper, corner-rounders (or just nail clippers and a credit card), transparencies, lamination pouches, rulers, and a lot of patience.

NOTES

1. These dpi statements are especially true for inkjet and laser printers, which I suspect most readers will be using. The Alps printer, which I discuss later, works wonders with images under 300 dpi when printing in dye-sublimation mode.
2. In practice, at the time of this writing, this seldom occurs. These numbers are given for demonstration. In truth, a 1,200-dpi scan from the Internet is quite common and usually sufficient to produce a believable fake. A 2,400-dpi scan in PhotoShop format would be a very big file—on the order of 5 megabytes or more, which is difficult to work with unless you own a very fast computer with lots of memory.
3. A top-ranking Internet auction service, eBay (www.ebay.com) is a great place to learn the true market value of almost any item in any condition.
4. Sheldon X. Charrett, *Identity, Privacy, and Personal Freedom: Big Brother vs. The New Resistance* (Boulder, CO: Paladin Press, 1999). For the typewriter list, see Chapter 3 of that text. For information on becoming an Irish citizen, see Chapter 5 of that text.

Section Two

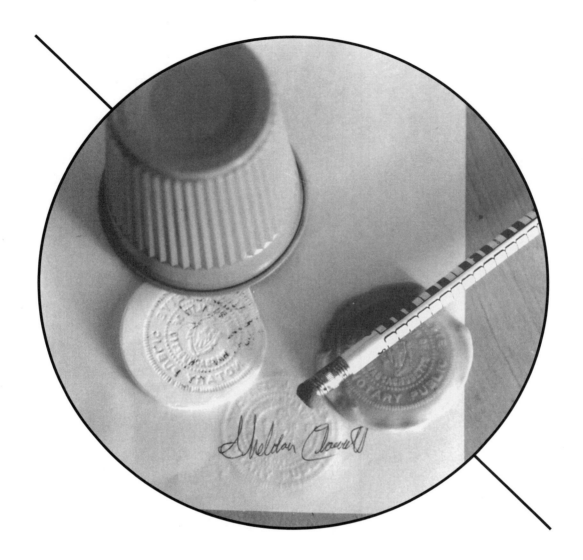

DOCUMENT SECURITY

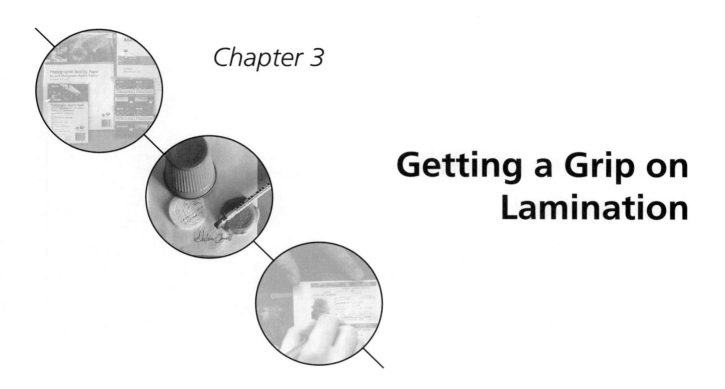

Getting a Grip on Lamination

Chapter 3

Hot lamination, cold lamination, 5 mil, 10 mil, polypropylene, vinyl chloride microlamination, poor man's lamination, and, finally, where do I get the stuff? While researching this book, I perused many Internet discussion boards and saw there were still quite a few people confused by lamination. As an ID professional, I'd conquered lamination long ago and had forgotten the days when it really had me buggered.

Lamination was one of the earliest document security devices. For a long time, laminators were available only to municipalities and large corporations, so as a security device they weren't half bad in their day. Even today people have trouble finding lamination pouches and laminators. Indeed, these topics comprise a large majority of the questions I encounter on the Web, and some of the discussion board answers are equally as telling. Respondents often suggest that the inquirer invent a company letterhead to facilitate buying lamination pouches from outfits that supply them. This demonstrates the strong air of authority still surrounding lamination today. Fortunately, lamination supplies are not nearly as difficult to get as people still seem to think. I'll list some sources at the end of this chapter.

If obtaining lamination supplies is not the problem, then what is? Actually, the modern document forger faces a few. There is the Shakespearean question of double-laminating, to do or not to do? There are blurring and fading issues when laminating over papers specially treated for certain desktop publishing processes. There is the problem of how lamination will affect the quality of a hologram. There are probably more problems (aren't there always?), but these are the ones that most affect document forgers and as such are the only ones discussed in this chapter.

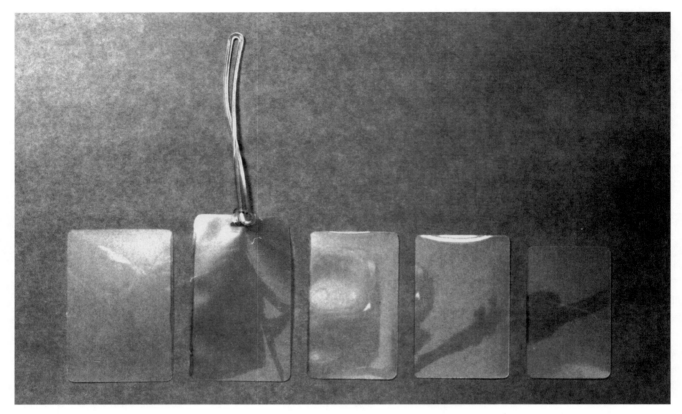

Various lamination pouches (from left to right): military card, luggage tag, business card, driver's license, and credit card.

First the basics. There are three words:

- *lamination*
- *laminate* (pronounced "lam in 8")
- *lamina*

These three words are constantly misused; at least as far as I can see on Internet discussion boards. To be sure that there's no confusion in this chapter, I'll define them here. *Lamination* refers to the *process* of enveloping something in plastic. *Laminate* is a verb; it is the *act* of encasing something in plastic. *Lamina* is the plastic sheet that covers something. The last word is where the trouble starts. Nobody uses it—at least not on the Internet. Rather they say *laminate* with an "it" sound (lam in it), or worse, *laminant*, which isn't a word. To prevent confusion, I'll use *lamination pouch* whenever I am referring to one. I'll use *lamina* when referring to a single layer of the pouch, especially after it has passed through the laminator.

Lamination pouches come in various sizes and thicknesses. They are usually rectangular, but the length of the rectangle varies depending on the pouch's intended use. Some intended uses are military, business, and credit cards; luggage tags; and driver's licenses. The military card and luggage tag pouches are larger than the credit card, business card, and driver's license pouches. The business card pouches are longer than the driver's license and credit card pouches.

A long driver's license, such as the New Jersey one we'll be building later, is actually best fitted into a business card pouch. A small driver's license is best fitted into a credit card pouch. Large driver's

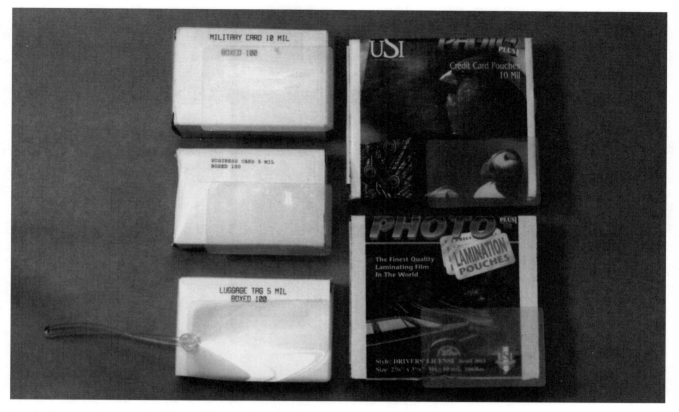

Lamination pouches come in 50- to 100-count boxes. They are available through USI, laminationstation.com, and office supply stores.

licenses fit nicely into the driver's license pouch, as do birth certificate abstracts, which we'll also be building later.

Luggage tag and military card pouches are good to have on hand. Either can be used to make an employment badge, student parking permit, etc. The 5-mil version makes a good first layer when double-laminating. Once the first layer's done you can trim it to size with a paper cutter before applying the second layer.

Lamination pouches are available in 5-mil and 10-mil thicknesses. *Mil* does not mean millimeter, nor does it mean millionths of an inch. Mil is from the Latin *mille,* meaning one thousand. It is where we get the word *millennium,* meaning 1,000 years; as well as *millisecond,* meaning one-thousandth of a second. It is also the root of the real estate term "mill rate," which is how much tax per thousand dollars of property value you send to your town hall every year if you own a home. Use these facts to remember that mil means one-thousandth of an inch. A 10-mil pouch is ten-thousandths (or one-hundredth) of an inch thick.

Five-mil pouches are good for the "no edge" style of laminated card, such as the early- to mid-1990s South Carolina driver's license, and the mid- to late-1990s Wyoming driver's license. They are also good when double-laminating, otherwise the finished ID is too thick.

DOUBLE-LAMINATING: TO DO OR NOT TO DO?

Document forgers consider many factors when deciding whether to double-laminate. Some forgers double-laminate solely because an ID printed to thin paper seems too thin if only single-laminated.

In a pinch, the poor man can use Super Clear cellophane tape as lamination. This tape also comes in handy when cold lamination is preferred, such as over diffractive holograms.

Some forgers like to apply a hologram or repetitive lettering pattern over a 5-mil laminated ID card and then relaminate with another 5-mil pouch to protect the hologram. The two principal disadvantages to double-laminating are (1) sometimes the ID comes out too thick, and (2) sometimes air pockets are introduced between the lamination layers.

It's up to you whether to double-laminate, and your decision will likely vary with the ID. As long as you know the pros and cons, you can make an educated decision.

HOW LAMINATION AFFECTS A HOLOGRAM

Lamination does not appear to have a detrimental effect on metallic-style holograms or repetitive lettering. However, there are a handful of eventualities one must consider when working with rainbow holograms. These will be discussed in the next section.

POOR MAN'S LAMINATION

If you can't afford a laminator, you can still make an academic study of modern document forgery. For a buck or two, many office superstores will laminate something for you. More often that not, there is an apathetic teenager who handles this end of the business, and he probably won't even notice or care what you're up to.

If you can afford (or otherwise obtain) lamination pouches, a heavy-bottomed skillet, clothes iron, and paper napkin can act as your laminator. Turn the iron on to its highest setting and rest it on an

A clothes iron, an upside-down saucepan, and napkin make a very effective laminator for the poor man.

upside-down skillet. You can also use an upside-down frying pan, saucepan, or anything that conducts and holds heat. After 5 minutes, the skillet should feel hot to the touch, even a few inches away from where the iron is resting. Your ID, back, hologram, whatever, should already be neatly arranged in a lamination pouch. Fold a paper napkin around the lamination pouch just like you're making a god-damn taco. Place the "taco" on the heated pan and press the iron on top of it. Rub the iron back and forth over the pouch for 5 to 10 seconds; then check the results. If you have to reapply the iron, first flip the ID so as not to overheat one side and then reapply for only a few seconds this time. I've found that reapplication is seldom necessary.

This method works so well that I've been tempted to put my laminator up for bid on eBay. In some ways, I prefer this method to using a laminator because you have more control over the finished product, and the end result is just as good as any laminator does. So, if you don't yet own a laminator, feel free to save yourself a hundred bucks by using this method.

If you're worried about heat lamination ruining your diffractive hologram (discussed in greater detail in the next section), you can use several layers of peel-and-stick lamination sheets or Super Clear tape.

A Word about Blurring

Laminating directly over a printed template may cause the finished ID to become blurred over time. I show an example of this effect on page 28.

The examples were printed on Alps photographic paper using the dye-sublimation process. It does not take very long for the blurring effect to show itself. Sometimes it appears within hours and only

It's somewhat difficult to see in this black and white photo, but if you look closely around the pseudo-typeface "Xavier Sabine Charrett" you will note a dark holo around the letters. The effect is severe and unacceptable. The color photograph on my Web site shows the effect in its full ignominy.

gets worse over time. In this case, Alps ink (actually a dye) sublimating back into the vinyl chloride coating of the lamination pouch caused the blurring.

A similar effect can occur when laminating directly over specially coated inkjet photo papers. The vinyl chloride in the lamination pouch interacts with the photo paper's substrate, which is a form of plastic. As the substrate deteriorates, the ink no longer has a dependable matrix onto which it can adhere. The ink spreads out and looks blurry.

No matter the cause, a blurred ID is a dead giveaway that it's a fake. So what do licentious larcenists do when they find themselves in this untenable situation? They redo the ID, placing a barrier between the photo paper and the lamination pouch. This, of course, opens a new can of worms because if you choose the wrong material, you will have air bubbles instead of fuzzy ink. A transparency sheet can sometimes do the trick, but occasionally an air bubble or two will form. A better bet is the HG-107 holographic film discussed later, which can serve two purposes if you also happen to need a hologram. Efficient.

AND FINALLY, WHERE DO I GET THE STUFF?

Here are two good sources for laminators and lamination supplies:

USI, Inc.
33 Business Park Drive, Suite 5
Branford, CT 06405-2944

Lamination Station
837 Miramar Street
Cape Coral, FL 33904
E-mail: Sales@laminationstation.com
Web: www.laminationstation.com

That's the lowdown on lamination. I've provided enough information to get you through the academic studies in this book. On some IDs, the last step before lamination is to insert your hologram. The next chapter discusses holograms in detail.

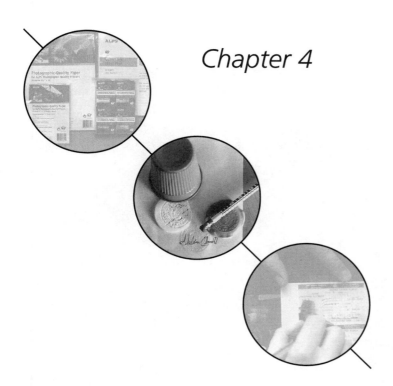

Chapter 4

Holograms

The term *hologram is* used to describe various optical effects, including those used in document security devices. In actuality, a hologram is a laser-generated recording of an object onto a holographic film. Unlike standard photography, a holograph stores the interference pattern of light waves reflected off an object. A standard photograph only records the color and intensity of light.

If this sounds complex, it is. If it sounds like more than you want to get involved with, don't worry. We are not going to get into making actual holograms—that would require between $3,000 and $30,000 worth of equipment. Rather, we are going to explore how recalcitrant reprobates create holographic effects on their fake IDs. In fact, some ID cards, including state driver's licenses, employ techniques very similar to those we'll be exploring. For our purposes, we will refer to these simulated holographic effects as holograms.

PIONEERING RESEARCH

The hologram most people write me about is the rainbow hologram. A rainbow hologram is the kind that's invisible when viewed at some angles and greenish or multicolored at other angles. Some methods of dealing with these holograms were presented in my last book.[1] I have this thing about rehashing: it's boring to write, and readers find it annoying to spend $35 on a book they've already read. So I'm not going to review those techniques in this text. Instead, I present some completely new techniques pioneered by myself and a few close members of my discussion board.[2] I especially want to thank Bill P., whose inspiration kept me from settling for second-rate holograms. He openly and

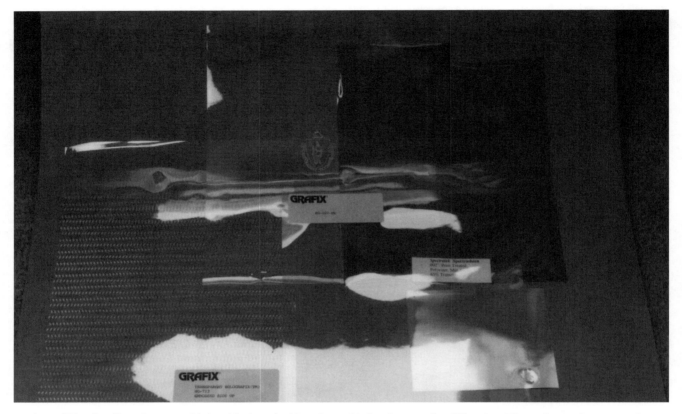

Various diffractive films. Because this is a black and white photo, it's hard to see the diffraction. The variegated areas on the curved sheet are actually beautiful rainbows.

generously shared his thorough and meticulous research and is largely responsible, in one way or another, for the material that follows.

DIFFRACTIVE FILM

To create a rainbow hologram you need a sheet of transparent film, such as extruded polyester, that has been treated on one side with a diffractive grating. A detailed study of diffractive gratings is hard physical science and well beyond the scope of this text. This discussion will be limited only to what you need to know to make a rainbow hologram on a novelty ID. If you are interested in the science of holograms and document security in general, I recommend *Optical Document Security,* published by Artech House Publishing and edited by Rudolf L. van Renesse.

There are a few things you need to know about diffractive film. A brief education will help you avoid costly mistakes and unnecessary repetition when incorporating "holos" into your novelty IDs. You'll also learn how low-caste crudballs use this same information to ensure that bureaucrats accept their IDs as genuine. Diffractive film holograms are not ideal in all lighting conditions, and crafty crooks know how to present them.

First, you must understand that there are different kinds of diffractive films. Illustration 1 (see page 36) shows a *surface relief* diffractive grating, which means the grating is etched onto the surface of the film. There are other microstructures, known as *buried microstructures,* where the diffractive grating is beneath the surface of the film. Those won't be discussed here.

You'll note that only one side of the film has the diffractive grating. It is the uniform spacing

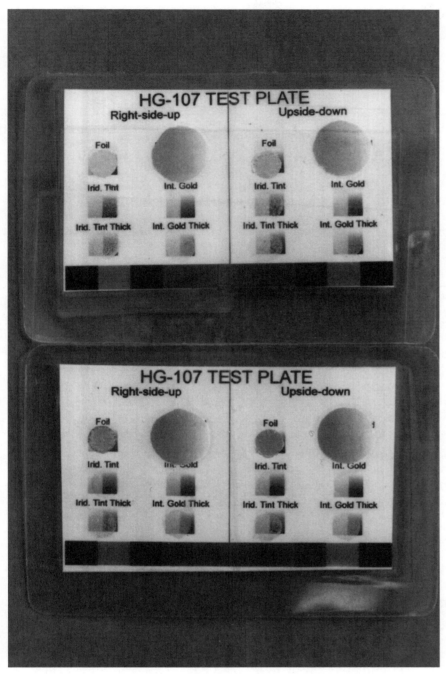

You can make a test plate to test the iridescence of a given film under varying circumstances. The top test plate tests HG-107 over aluminum foil, Gold Metallic (Alps) ink, iridescent tinting medium, and Interference Gold acrylic paint. I tested the film against the tinting medium and Interference Gold in thin and heavy applications. The plate is laminated with the HG-107 right side up on the left and upside down on the right. The test plate also tests iridescence against five colors along the bottom (brown, tan, blue, green, red). The bottom test plate tests the effects of adding a "buffer layer" of HG-107 to protect the gratings from vinyl chloride in the lamination pouch.

between the grates that causes light to be refracted into all the colors of the rainbow. In fact, it is the same type of uniform alignment of water molecules in the atmosphere that causes real rainbows. For our discussion, you don't need to know why this happens. Just be aware that light is diffracted because of the gratings and that the gratings are only on one side of the film. Later on, it will be very important to keep track of which side has the gratings.

So How Do I Get the Stuff?

You can't just walk into a store and say, "Hey, can I get a sheet of transparent extruded polyester that has been treated on one side with a diffractive grating?" The clerk will call the men in white coats on you. Nor can you approach a manufacturer of such industrial-grade material and ask for $2 worth. The manufacturer will inform you that the minimum order it accepts is 20,000 square feet. Diffractive film is usually sold in bulk to other manufacturers who use it to make fancy packaging for their products. In recent years, you've probably seen diffractive film on toothpaste boxes and magazine covers, among other places.

So the only way to get the stuff is to be a manufacturer considering the use of diffractive film in your packaging . . . or to say that you are. Call,

TABLE 1: RESULTS OF HG-107 EXPERIMENT

HG-107 TEST PLATE SINGLE LAYER OF DIFFRACTIVE FILM		HG-107 TEST PLATE TWO LAYERS OF DIFFRACTIVE FILM TO TEST BUFFER EFFECT			
RIGHT SIDE UP	UPSIDE DOWN	RIGHT SIDE UP		UPSIDE DOWN	
(NO SECOND LAYER)		RIGHT-SIDE-UP BUFFER	UPSIDE-DOWN BUFFER	RIGHT-SIDE-UP BUFFER	UPSIDE-DOWN BUFFER
Effect completely destroyed due to vinyl chloride clogging the grating.	Effect present but diminished over dark colors (brown, tan, blue, green, red).	Effect present and somewhat better over dark colors. Hypotheses: (1) a buffer layer will protect the HG-107 gratings, (2) buffered gratings are better than upside-down gratings possibly because (a) the active gratings do not react with the template, (b) the active layer has added protection from heat lamination via the buffer layer.	Air bubbles formed in between gratings in the HG-107 layers because there was no "escape route." An HG-107 buffer layer should be placed right side up.	Buffer somewhat superfluous because HG-107 was already protected by being upside down. Produced about equal results. Buffer layer may help protect active layer from heat lamination.	
Notes: In all cases where the effect was present, the foil produced the strongest rainbow due to its high reflectivity. The Interference Gold produced the second strongest rainbow, but since the foil is less practical, the Interference Gold is the real winner. The iridescent tinting medium showed promise and may be valuable in future experiments. It should be noted that the white background in itself provided sufficient reflectivity to produce the effect. The solid colors are definitely a problem, and the ID forger will have to watch his backgrounds. Interestingly enough, however, shiny black lines produced high reflectivity in separate experiments.					

write, or e-mail a company that makes holographic packaging material and ask for samples. I'm not going to publish a list of companies here for these reasons:

- If all my readers go to the same company, the company will get suspicious and begin investigating inquiries before sending samples.
- Future industrial supply startups will be eager to grow their business by handing out samples. These are the companies you should seek out, but I have no way of knowing now which ones they'll be.

That said, I'm going to show you a product that meets our needs—but only to a certain extent. It will be good enough to demonstrate the process, but not so good that everybody will run to this manufacturer and spoil the source. If you're truly interested in seeing the effect in all its glory, then you'll have to seek out a film with a higher diffractive index in the zero order (hint, hint, hint). Okay?

HG-107 Has Merit

HG-107 is a film I experimented with that produced wonderful effects in direct light but failed to meet the mark in diffuse light (such as the ambient light of an overcast day). This is because its grating microstructure has a "first-order" readout (not as good as "zero order" hint, hint. (See Chapter 12 of *Optical Document Security*, cited on page 32.) Nonetheless, a document forger can use HG-107 or equivalent in certain situations.

I Have Diffractive Film—Now What?

Diffractive film won't itself produce a hologram. It needs a reflective material underneath it to send light back to the viewer's eye. In many cases, the reflective material can simply be the ID template itself. Or it can be something like Interference Gold acrylic paint. If the paint is applied in the

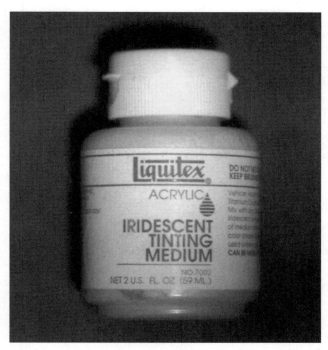

Though not discussed further in this text, the iridescent tinting medium showed promise as a reflective substance.

shape of a state's hologram . . . well . . . then things start to get interesting.

Reread the above paragraph a couple of times. It is the crux of this entire section.

PUTTING IT ALL TOGETHER IN AN ID

Because the diffractive grating produces the holographic effect, you must be careful not to destroy it when constructing the novelty ID. This may sound obvious, but the grating is very delicate and there are many things that can affect it during the construction process. The grating's biggest enemy is heat lamination. The vinyl chloride in the lamination pouch can clog the grating and destroy the holographic effect (see Table 1 on previous page). The heat of the laminator is also a problem because it can melt the polyester and distort the grating. Even a slightly distorted grating will affect the overall holographic effect. Any melting at all will change the size, shape, and uniformity of the grating microstructure, all of which affect its ability to diffract light.

You can protect the grating from becoming clogged with vinyl chloride by adding another layer of film over it, a buffer layer. If another layer of diffractive film is used, the gratings of both layers should be facing up. (Refer to Illustration 1, page 36.)

The illustration shows five layers. The bottom layer is the ID card itself. The next "layer" up is the reflective material, such as Interference Gold paint. In reality, this won't be much of a layer, but it is shown as one for clarity. Over that is the first layer of diffractive film with the gratings facing up. I'll call this the "active" layer since it is the one that produces the holographic effect. A second layer of film is placed over the active layer to protect the grating from the vinyl chloride in the lamination pouch and direct heat of the laminator. In reality, the film in this layer need not contain diffractive gratings. But since you already have the product on hand, you might as well use it. I like using it anyway because the gratings (which should be facing up) give the vinyl chloride somewhere to go during lamination. In fact, in my HG-107 experiment I proved that this arrangement produces the fewest air bubbles. If you were to place the top (or "passive") layer of film upside down over the active layer, air would be trapped between the gratings as well as just underneath the lamina. The vinyl chloride in the lamination pouch should be absorbed by a porous substrate, such as paper. Therefore, using a surface relief diffractive film over the first layer proves to be an effective solution all around.[3]

CAVEATS

Reproducing holograms with diffractive film carries a general caveat because diffractive film is really not a hologram. Using a first-order film such as HG-107 carries additional caveats. As previously mentioned, first-order grating microstructures need a direct light source to produce a hologram. This means your novelty ID will have little or no hologram if presented outdoors on an overcast day.

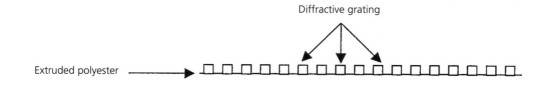

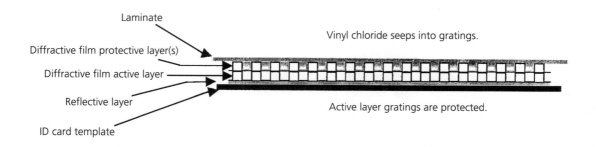

Illustration 1 shows the various layers of a diffractive film hologram ID. It shows a second layer of film to protect the first and a reflective layer beneath the first layer of film. It is possible to have only one layer of film, an "active" layer, upside down and cold-laminated (or very carefully heat-laminated). Also, the reflective layer need not be a separate metallized layer. A glossy template may have sufficient reflectivity without metallization.

The opposite is also true. Certain direct lighting conditions will cause the ID to show a hologram where you don't want one. If the ID card has an area that is highly reflective, such as shiny black lettering, small, unwanted holograms can pop up in direct light. For this reason, you must take care when designing the card so that no highly reflective areas exist except where you want them. Or you can use the following technique for placing a design directly onto diffractive film.

PLACING A DESIGN ON DIFFRACTIVE FILM

You can eliminate unwanted holograms by purposely clogging the diffractive grating where holograms are not needed. You do this by coating the active layer of diffractive film with clear gloss artist's finishing spray or equivalent. You can carry this concept one step further to place a complete design directly onto the film. Again, special thanks to Bill P. for the following procedure. You will need the following:

- Diffractive film (embossed side identified)
- Latex paste or latex masking fluid
- Clear gloss artist's finishing spray
- Stencil of design

Except for the diffractive film, you should be able to get everything you need from a good art supplies source. You will have to engage in some trial and error to find the right sort of finishing spray. Read the ingredients and avoid anything containing acetone or other organic solvents. Acetone reacts with most plastics and will turn the film white. I've used Grumbacher "advanced formula" damar varnish "gloss" (catalog #645), which worked well.[4] A decent masking fluid is Grumbacher *Miskit*™ Liquid Frisket. I purchased both Grumbacher products at Ben Franklin Crafts.

Paladin horsehead logo cut from low-tack tape placed on license-size piece of HG-107 diffractive film. The right side of the film has been clogged with damar varnish as described in this section. You can see the difference between the right (clogged) and left (unclogged) sides. To drive home this point, I sprayed a cotton swab with the varnish and wrote "TEST" on the otherwise unclogged left half of the film.

Procedure

This procedure will work on any surface relief diffractive grating film. Depending on how fancy you want to get, the stencil can be cut at home from card, Mylar, Dura-Lar, or frisk film, or cut by a laser cutting service from Mylar, vinyl, or metal. Unless you get involved with a laser cutting service, the following procedure is more "old school" than you might expect, considering that we're replicating a hologram.

1. Place stencil over embossed side of diffractive film.[5] Fasten securely, ensuring that there are no gaps between the stencil and the film, and sandwich them tightly. This is where vinyl, Mylar, Dura-Lar, and metal are better than card.
2. If using latex paste, then apply carefully over exposed areas of stencil with a small spatula. If using liquid latex, use a brush. I think applying the liquid latex with a brush is more controlled.
3. Allow this to dry. When dry, latex forms a thin and flexible rubber that you will later be able to peel off.
4. Carefully remove the stencil. Use a scalpel or hobby knife, if necessary. You should have a latex-covered version of the design.
5. In a well-ventilated area, lay the film flat and apply finishing spray. You can spray the film directly or spray the corner of a very clean, lint-free cloth and rub the finish into the film. If rubbing, be careful not to rub off the latex mask during this step. You are trying to clog the grating. The amount of finishing spray required will vary depending on the type of film and the spray itself. Experiment to find the technique that suits you best.
6. Allow finishing spray to dry.
7. Use adhesive tape or a soft rubber eraser to begin peeling the latex. Use your fingers or a pair of tweezers to peel the remainder.

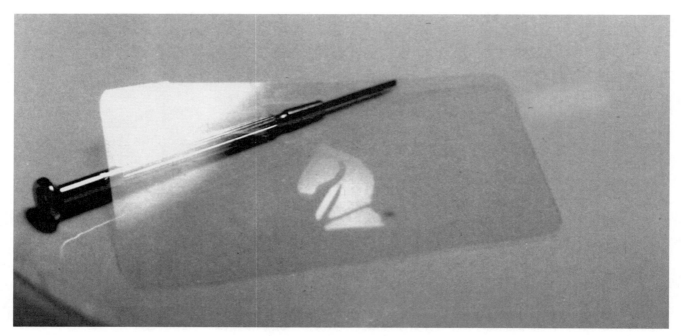

After the film was completely clogged, I allowed the varnish to dry and then peeled back the low-tack tape. Use the tip of your stencil knife to lift a corner of the tape (or frisk film) to start the peel. The Paladin horsehead hologram was now ready to be used in an ID.

Here it is shown over a darker background. It's a little blurry 'cause the FBI was knocking at my door and my hand was shaking. Why is it refracting light with no reflective surface behind it? This is an inherent property of the HG-107. A reflective surface is needed only when there is a surface, such as when the holo is placed over an ID card.

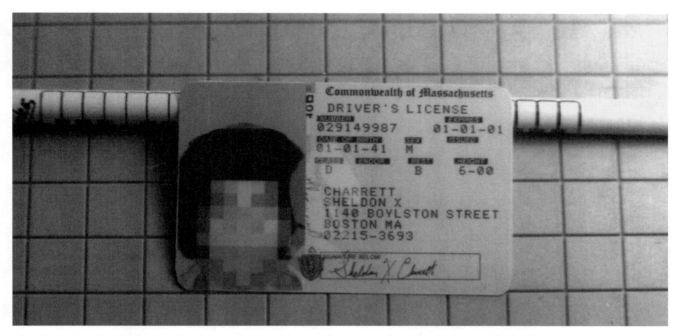

Here is the horsehead hologram facedown on a Massachusetts license template. The damar varnish doubles as a glue, helping the diffractive film adhere to the ID template. This also protects the active surface (gratings) from lint, hairs, fingerprints, etc. The exposed (nongrating) side is smooth, so any fingerprints left during construction can be easily wiped away with a lint-free cloth.

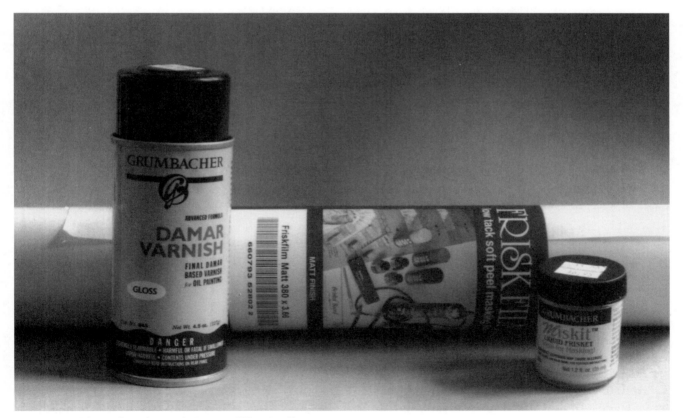

Some materials used to place a design on diffractive film.

8. You should now have a diffractive hologram seemingly embedded inside a piece of clear plastic. When done right, it looks quite impressive.

Alternative Technique

Liquid latex can be a real pain to work with. If you lack artistic skill or patience, you can use this alternate technique. Instead of steps 2, 3, and 4 substitute the following:

Cut a "positive" design (as opposed to a stencil) of your hologram into frisk film, such as the type shown in the photo shown on page 37. Apply the positive design to the diffractive film before clogging the gratings. Once the gratings are sufficiently clogged and the finishing spray is dry, carefully peel the design from the diffractive film. This also yields impressive results. (See the preceding photo series.)

Thermal Scribing

The foregoing methods for placing a design on diffractive film work quite nicely if the design is not too complex. But what about more intricate designs, such as the California or Massachusetts hologram? Hiring a laser cutting service to make a stencil for one ID is not very cost-effective. What's a nefarious necromancer to do? Well, if you don't mind playing Russian roulette with your Alps print head, you can print a negative of any image you'd like directly onto the embossed side of any surface relief diffractive film.

By printing the negative image in dye-sublimation mode, you are actually using the heat of the print head to melt unwanted areas of the grating microstructure. When done, only the areas you want to diffract will remain. It doesn't matter how intricate the design is; it's just like printing a graphic.

So what's the problem? Well, there's a good chance you'll damage your print head and an even better chance you'll damage the ink cartridge ribbon. In fact, I would say damage is likely unless you "print" to the film one pass at a time, allowing the print head to cool in between each pass. You would need several files, each a different "row" of the image, and it would probably be best to "print" in the lightest shade of yellow so that no actual ink makes it to the film.

I will not provide step-by-step instructions because I don't think you should attempt this method. I tried it with my Alps, and the yellow ribbon fused to the HG-107 on the second pass. My heart sank, and I promised God that if the print head was undamaged I would be a good boy for the rest of my life. Lucky for me, the print head was not damaged. Keeping my promise to God, I did not attempt this again.

I share this information with you only because there are other types of thermal printers in the world that will fare much better with this method. Buy cheap ones in the government surplus market and experiment. Share your results with others on my Web site so they'll know exactly how moronic marauders (of whom we are making an academic study) do this sort of thing and to steer clear of such anarchy.

METALLIZATION

Using the above techniques, you may be quite amazed by the quality of the "hologram" seemingly embedded in the diffractive film. It is a rather impressive sight, especially if you've ever thought a hologram's presence precluded you from reproducing a given ID. You may get so excited that you stuff the holo into a lamination pouch along with a template and back. But as soon as you run it through the laminator all your high hopes crumble into a pile of disappointment. What went wrong? You protected the grating, you didn't overheat your laminator, you did everything right . . . but your results are marginal or nonexistent.

Actually, doing all of the above sometimes yields excellent results—*sometimes*. But I wouldn't count on it. To ensure that your hologram shines through, you'll need something highly reflective beneath it to bounce light back through the hologram and up to the viewer's eye. That's when the magic happens.

Certain ID templates may be inherently reflective. Other times it is better to provide a small amount of metallization underneath the hologram to ensure a holographic effect.

Use the "Poor Man's N.J. Holo" method (described in Chapter 3 of *Identity, Privacy, and Personal Freedom: Big Brother vs. the New Resistance*) to place a near-invisible amount of Interference Gold paint directly onto the ID template where a hologram. That should do it. If you come up with other methods or refinements to this method, please visit my discussion board and share it (see the Appendix).

NOTES

1. Charrett, *Identity, Privacy, and Personal Freedom: Big Brother vs. The New Resistance.*
2. You can link to my discussion board from my Web site http://www.phreak.co.uk/sxc. (Please see the Appendix for more information about finding me on the Web.)
3. Buried microstructure films will not exhibit this quality.
4. M. Grumbacher, Inc. is a U.S. company headquartered in Bloomsbury, N.J. Its damar varnish product contains gum spirits of turpentine, heptane, isobutan-propane mixture, isopropyl alcohol, and prime damar resin.
5. When ordering sample material, ask the sales representative to label the embossed side. The embossed side of the HG-107 film is the side that reacts more strongly to your fingerprints. Other surface relief microstructures may also exhibit this characteristic.

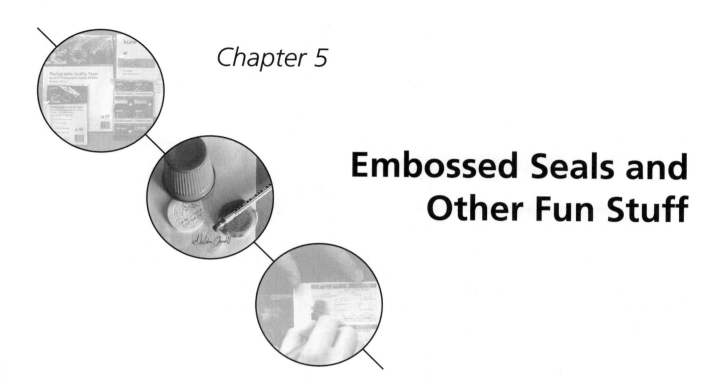

Chapter 5

Embossed Seals and Other Fun Stuff

This chapter is an academic study of how unmutual underworld overlords forge embossed seals, such as those found on notarized legal instruments. An embossed seal adds a nice touch to certain identity documents as well. For example, a state-issued marriage certificate is usually embossed with a state seal. A city-issued birth certificate abstract usually has a city seal embossed smack dab in the middle. An application for voluntary administration of an estate (not ID exactly, but it can come in handy) usually requires a notary's seal at the bottom.

I've also included a small section on bar codes, ultraviolet-sensitive ink, and magnetic swipes.

EMBOSSED SEAL

I must first point out that you could borrow an unguarded embosser to "officially" notarize something. Many ID books correctly suggest you can find various stamps, seals, and embossers at yard sales and flea markets. I agree: keep an eye out so you can see where lawless larcenists buy such unspeakable contraband. You could also use forged credentials to get a fake driver's license, which will allow you to notarize any document you'd like in your fake name. But this is a book about how good-for-nothing bastard criminals manufacture and forge ID documents, so we'll just skip all those tricks and get right to the nuts-and-bolts, hands-on document forgery methods used by modern-day cretins and crackpots.

Depending on your desired level of quality, you could forge a notary's seal in several ways:

- Silver dollar method
- Amusement park coin method
- Wood block, etching, and sand carving method
- I Love Super Sculpey™ method

Silver-Dollar Method

Using a silver dollar and a rubber mallet (or shoe) is a quick way to lend the impression of an embossed seal. Lay your document over a silver dollar and then smash it with a rubber mallet—voilà!—a raised seal. It is preferable to use a Morgan dollar to an Eisenhower dollar because the former is less familiar and reduces the chance of catching somebody's eye. Also be careful not to do too good a job. Basically, all you want is the edges and a wee bit of surface area to emboss the paper. You do not want the words "ONE DOLLAR" to stand out, or your little ploy will be for naught. Delinquent dolts use this method to add a genuine touch to hospital birth records passed off to low-level clerks (or medium-level clerks with thick glasses).

Amusement Park Coin Method

Amusement parks, arcades, and novelty greeting card shops sometimes have a machine that allows you type your name or other statement on a coin. Teenagers usually write things like "MARY LOVES JOHNNY 4-EVA" and "BLINK182 KICKS ASS." Document forgers, however, write things like "JAMES DEAN—NOTARY PUBLIC" or "NOTARY PUBLIC—NOTARY PUBLIC" or "CITY OF SAINT LOUIS." You get the idea. They then use the previously outlined silver-dollar method to "notarize" documents. A money launderer might use this method to notarize an "Application for Voluntary Administration" of a 50-year-old unprobated estate. The forthcoming probate court certificate combined with a fake driver's license looks very convincing to the account specialist at a local bank. Mo-fo's move molto mullah through estate bank accounts in exactly this way.

Wood Block, Etching, and Sand Carving Method

If you have a tiny router or engraving tool, you can make your own seal out of wood. Simply draw, paint, print, transfer, or stencil the design onto a piece of hardwood, such as maple, ash, beech, or oak cut from a pristine area of the main tree trunk. Do not use softwood, such as pine, or your hours of effort will be good for only one or two embossings. Use a small router[1] or engraving tool with a Dremel bit to rout it out. You could even use a sharp hobby knife if you're careful and patient.

More serious identity crooks make a photo-resist stencil of the seal and sand carve it using a special artist's tool. Such tools are dropping in price and becoming more portable and easier to use. Keep your eye out for portable sand carvers and accessories if you're serious about experimenting with homemade seals.

These processes may seem rather elaborate, but keep in mind that in days of old the king's royal seal was made out of wood and they did not have access to routers, etching tools, photo-resist stencils, and sand carvers.

I Love Super Sculpey Method

Crafty grafters know about a nifty little product called Super Sculpey, available at any decent arts and crafts store. Sculpey is special sculpting putty that I've adapted to a special use. You can press Sculpey onto a three-dimensional object to make a perfect mold of it. Alternatively, you can press Sculpey into a mold to replicate a three-dimensional object. Hmmm. Big froinkin' deal, Charrett, I'm skipping ahead to the next chapter.

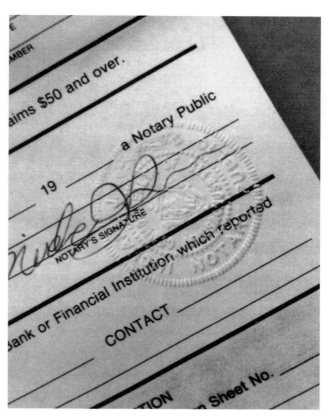

Notary embossed document seen from behind for clarity. Notice how this is a good, full impression. Some notaries have weak hands and give you lame impressions that aren't good enough for duplicating with the Super Sculpey method.

This is the same document as seen from the front. A silicone mold must be made from the front of a document.

Wait! You have to let me tell you why I Love Super Sculpey! Bear with me.

A notary's embossing plate is a three-dimensional object, right? So, if you are lucky enough to be alone with a notary's embosser for a few minutes, you could use Sculpey to make a mold of it.

Well, gee, thanks, Charrett, when in hell will I ever be alone with a notary's embosser? You suck.

Now wait a minute there, cowboy, those is harsh words. The good news is that we ordinary schmucks—the ones who'll never have a snowball's chance in hell of ever being alone with a notary's embosser—can use Sculpey in a different way.

Although you wouldn't normally think of it as such, the impression an embosser makes onto a piece of paper is actually a mold, innit? Certainly even we poor schmucks have a notarized document *somewhere* in our house. No? Well then, it's a simple matter to go the city clerk's office and get something notarized. Make sure the notary squeezes that embosser tight so you have a nice mold to work from. Tell him or her that you need a strong impression so it shows up on the photocopy.

When you get home, take a 3/4-inch ball of Super Sculpey and work it in your hands until it is very warm, soft, and pliable. Then press the Sculpey into the *back* of the embossed seal. Gently pull the paper from the Sculpey to reveal your new notary embossing plate. Bake it in the oven at 270 degrees for 15 minutes.[2] Serves one. Recipe may be doubled if you are expecting guests.

Once you pull Sculpey from the oven, let it cool for a couple hours. After that, your embossing plate should be hard and ready for service.

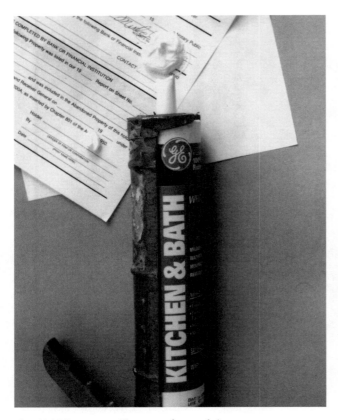

Apply 100-percent silicone to front of document.

Use a disposable cup to press silicone into the notary impression. Do this gently and don't over-squish. Let it set for at least 24 hours.

Peel the paper from the dried silicone. Rub off the paper residue in warm soapy water. You now have a very durable mold of a notary seal.

Silicone molds of Connecticut, Massachusetts, and New York notary seals.

Press a warm ball of Sculpey into the mold. Do this as evenly as possible. You'll have to press harder than when you squished the silicone onto the paper, but you still don't want to flatten it completely.

Peel the mold from the Sculpey. Place the ceramic cup with Sculpey into the oven (see procedure above).

Reusable Silicone Mold

There are two drawbacks to making a Sculpey embossing plate directly from a paper mold:

- The action of pressing into the paper causes you to lose some "edge" to the finished product.
- A deeply embossed paper will most likely tear when you pull the Sculpey from it. Thus you end up "breaking the mold."

Wouldn't it be nice to create a reusable mold? You can find all sorts of mold-making products in an arts and crafts store, usually in the $10 to $20 range. But none of them work as well as a $2 tube of kitchen and bath silicone sealant, which you can get from your local hardware store or the nearest Home Depot.

Simply squirt some silicone sealant on top of the notary's seal on the *front* of the page. Press the bottom of a plastic drinking cup onto it to get a good impression. Leave it sit overnight. The next day, gently peel the cup off the cured sealant. Then, even more gently, peel the paper from the sealant. Some of the paper will stick, but don't sweat it. Let it dry a couple more hours now that the ends are exposed to the air. Later on, wash out your mold with warm, soapy water. Don't be afraid to use a little elbow grease when cleaning; the silicone is quite durable. Once done, you can press Sculpey into the mold to create as many embossing plates as you want.

By the way, if you do happen to be left alone overnight with a notary's embosser, you can use the silicone method to create a reusable mold of the positive plate. Just a thought.

As you'll note from the photos above, I pressed the silicone mold into the Sculpey on the bottom of a ceramic coffee cup. I used the flat bottom of a drinking glass as a press. This helps ensure that the finished product is flat rather than wavy or bumpy. Keeping it flat will make better impressions and will help it last longer. The ceramic cup stayed with the Sculpey during baking. You *do not* want to peel the Sculpey and then place it in the oven. Peeling first would only distort it.

Cook Sculpey as described earlier.

How to Use the Sculpey Embosser

The best way to use your embosser is to carefully impress documents with a very soft pencil eraser. Place the document over the Sculpey embosser and use a soft pencil eraser to emboss the paper a little at a time. You can leave the Sculpey on the ceramic cup if you'd like, which would provide the strongest base for it since this is where the embosser was "born," and the cup's contours match those of the embosser.

OTHER FUN STUFF

Innovators of new ID often feel tripped up by ultraviolet-sensitive ink, magnetic swipes, bar codes, fingerprints, and other harbingers of tyranny—or rather, as we stand-up citizens prefer, necessary tools to control the masses.

Some driver's licenses are stamped on the back with special ink that shows up under ultraviolet (UV) light. Usually the stamp is the state's logo or some glib saying, such as "Just Say No." Shameless sinners replicate this security device with UV-sensitive fluid readily available in art supply stores or office/specialty supply sites on the Internet. Certain types of highlighters have been rumored to do the trick as well.

Bar codes are now easily generated with personal computers, and there's even a shareware program that produces encrypted bar codes, which look remarkably like the real thing (such as on an Arizona driver's license), though it probably doesn't use the same encryption scheme as the Arizona Department of Motor Vehicle (DMV). Bar code fonts are also available on compact disk or via Internet download. Of course, the gifted artist could surely draw a few lines of varying thickness to imitate a bar code.

Take the cup and Sculpey out of the oven and let cool for an hour or so. You now have your own notary embosser. Since this is only an academic study, you must now destroy it.

Hey! Didn't I tell you to destroy the embosser? Oh, well, if you absolutely must know, here's how bad people abuse Sculpey embossers. Place the document over the embosser and then impress it with a soft eraser.

48

Looky, looky. What do we have here?

Photo of the embosser, the embossing implement, and the finished product.

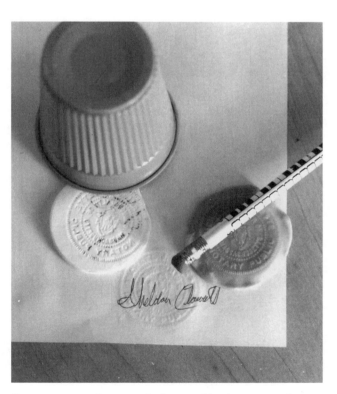

From paper to silicone to Sculpey and back to paper. Fun, fun, fun. Now destroy that embosser like I told you!

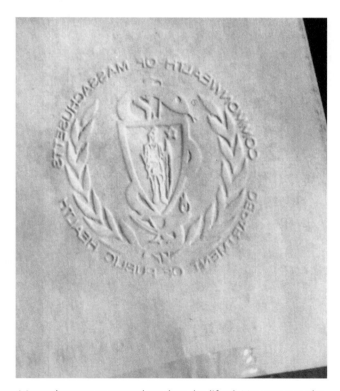

Massachusetts great seal ready to be lifted. You can use the foregoing Super Sculpey method to lift an embossed state seal and make an embosser from the mold.

Magnetic-ready PVC (CR-80) cards are available from printing supply companies, and both Eltron and Fargo make printers that can print, laminate, and encode the magnetic stripe on PVC cards. These printers are now selling for under $10,000.

The foregoing are just some random ideas that I may expand upon in a future book. But I have to draw the line somewhere on security devices because things are changing as we speak. If I were to go into details on everything, this book would never get to print. I've given you the current crème de la crème. The top security hurdle for ID forgers will soon be something else. Smart cards? Microchips embedded in the cerebellum? Bar codes tattooed on our feet at birth? Who knows? It's all possible. You can rest assured that our government is exploring all of these possibilities . . . for our own safety, of course.

Big Brother is looking out for us.

NOTES

1. In actual practice a router is only good for cleaning out the larger areas of the design, even when using the smallest bit. The details will have to be handled with an etching tool or a stencil knife.

2. These are the directions on the package. Don't use these settings in a Toast-R-Oven because the heating elements are too close to the Sculpey and it will boil. In practice, I've found that a much lower setting (150–170 degrees) for a longer time is more effective. Also, don't get Sculpey wet before baking. Sculpey no likey wet wet.

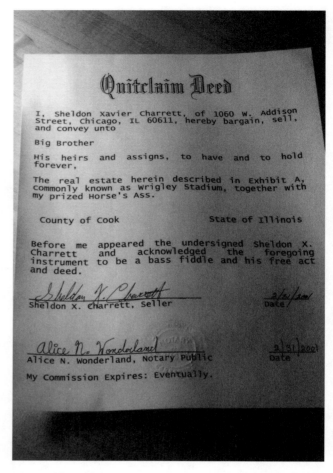

I just sold Wrigley Stadium and my prized horse's ass to Big Brother. Do you think he'll notice Alice N. Wonderland has her commission in Connecticut, and that the document was signed on February 31? Too bad we had to pixelate the notary's surname. It was a very nice print!

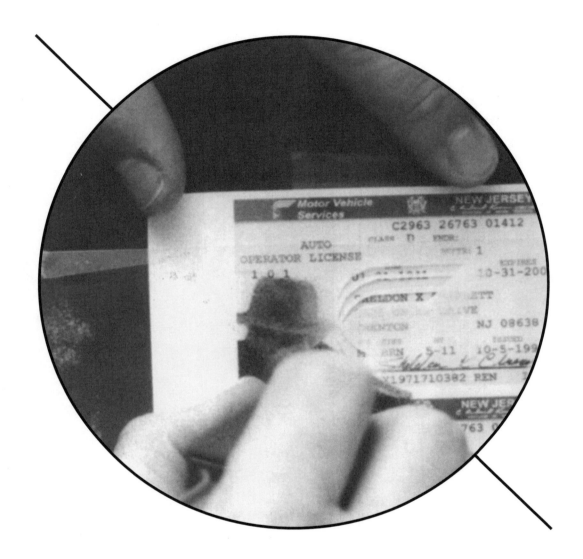

PUTTING IT ALL TOGETHER

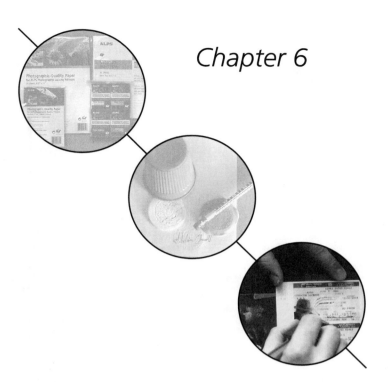

Chapter 6

Birth Certificates Made Easy

Author's note: I've laid out this section to provide a thorough examination of the various tools and techniques ID forgers use. To eliminate redundancy I've selected diverse documents, each highlighting a specific technique or process.

Forging original hospital-issued birth certificates is rife with problems. The document forger must find the appropriate paper, which is often no longer manufactured. Forgeries of this kind often involve the services of a professional printer to get the right ink effect and typesetting. This obviously limits the forger's possibilities unless he is a pressman by trade or trusts one with his freedom. A good replica must be properly aged. There are myriad solutions to these hurdles, but they seldom lend a natural effect.

Good solutions have been presented in other texts, and such information is invaluable. But how many people still have their original hospital birth certificates? And of those who do, how many carry them around for identification? More often, a person carries a city-issued abstract record of birth.

ABSTRACT RECORD OF BIRTH

Go to the town in which you were born and ask at the appropriate agency (e.g., city or county clerk's office) for a copy of your birth certificate. Most clerks will look up the certificate and type the vital information onto a card. They emboss the card with the city seal, laminate, collect $4 from you, and hand you an abstract record of birth. This card is what most people carry in their wallets as a birth certificate.

Fortunately for document forgers, this card is much easier to reproduce than a birth certificate.

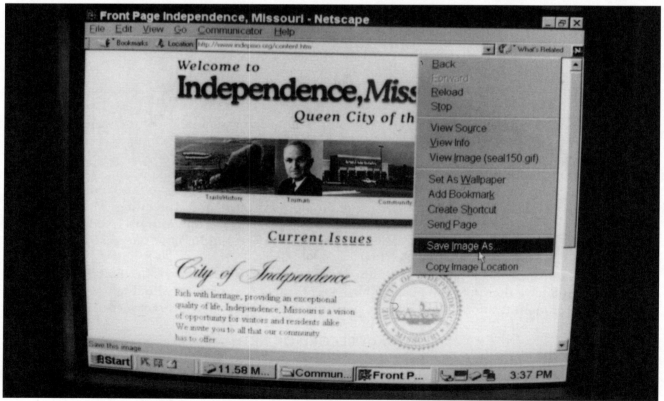

Not only is this record an abstract, it is completely surreal. I've never been to Independence, nor have I any idea what that town's abstracts look like. The Independence, Missouri, seal was taken from the city's Web site, shrunk down in PhotoShop, and pasted into its own layer.

PROCEDURE

These are the steps used by the criminal element to forge birth certificate abstracts.

- Design template
- Steal city seal
- Attest
- "Type in" vital statistics
- Print
- Emboss with city seal
- Laminate

Design Template

You can use the format in the top photo on page 54, or you can base your template on your target city's actual format from the year the record was supposedly made.[1] The heading font used in the above abstract is Old English Text MT. This is a wonderfully useful font, and I suggest you download it from the Internet or get it from a friend's computer if you don't already have it.

Steal City Seal

Use a scanner to scan a document containing your city's seal or, if your city has a Web site, download the image from there. You want a black and white version only. Once imported into PhotoShop, choose: Select, Color Range, Shadows. This will select only the black areas. Copy this and paste it into its own layer. You now have a copy of the city seal that can be imported into other documents.

Attest

Now, make an "Attest" signature. You can invent one yourself and scan it into your computer, or you can hijack a signature from somewhere else—even a scanned copy of an actual birth record or abstract. Use the above PhotoShop technique to isolate the signature from its background.

"Type In" Vital Statistics

The abstract record in the top photo on page 54 has no actual typing on it. Make a vital stats layer using the font Courier New, which is a good "typewriter" font. Once done, select the entire layer using the marquee tool and choose Image, Rotate, Arbitrary, and type in 1 degree. It does not matter whether you rotate 1-degree clockwise or counterclockwise. This lends the effect of a preprinted card that has been manually fed into a typewriter. Most of us have experienced this when filling in a form with a typewriter—the form never feeds in "level" no matter how hard we try. One degree of "unlevelness" implies authenticity.

Print

Once done with tweaking the template and vital info, print it out. This is a simple step, but one that must be considered carefully. Will you be adding a seal to the card? If so, what technique will you be using? If you have access to your city's embosser, then go ahead and print the abstract onto a heavy stock card, such as Alps photo paper. If you'll be using the I Love Super Sculpey Method (see Chapter 5), then you'll be better off printing the abstract onto a thinner paper, such as HammerMill Laser Paper, which can be readily embossed using that method.

Emboss with City Seal

You can often get away with omitting this step because many clerks don't know to look for it. This stems from the fact that each city does things differently. This is changing as Big Brother moves toward interjurisdictional standardization, but it will still be decades before all cities share a common policy.

Even though it is thick, the Alps photo-quality paper can be embossed using the Sculpey method. The embossing looks faint, but this is often the case with real documents anyway. Surprisingly, despite the thinness of the Alps VPhoto paper, it cannot be embossed due to its composition. These are things a good crook needs to keep in mind.

Laminate

It is best to buy or borrow a professional laminator for this step. Remember that certain inkjet photo papers will react with the vinyl chloride in the lamination pouch, as will the Alps photo paper. In these cases, you'll need a protective layer between the lamination pouch and the card.

STATE "LONG FORM" RECORD OF BIRTH

Birth certificates issued by state vital records offices are often legal-sized photocopies with the state's great seal embossed at the bottom. Bureaucrats affectionately refer to these as "long forms." (They must've reached into their magic sack of creativity to come up with that term.) Unlike abstracts, you do not carry around a long form in your wallet. Bureaucrats request the long form when, for example, you need to prove your Irish ancestry upon applying for

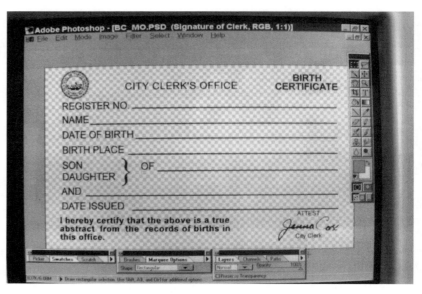

Template of birth certificate abstract with imported city seal in its own layer.

The USI FX-400 is a sturdy and dependable heat laminator. USI's current comparable models sell for between $50 and $130 new. I saw a used model on eBay with an opening bid of $5.

Form R-56
50M-8/95

The Commonwealth of Massachusetts
EXECUTIVE OFFICES OF HEALTH AND HUMAN SERVICES
STATE DEPARTMENT OF PUBLIC HEALTH
REGISTRY OF VITAL RECORDS AND STATISTICS

A 012345

I, the undersigned, hereby certify that I am the Registrar of Vital Records and Statistics; that as such I have custody of the records of birth, marriage and death required by law to be kept in my office; and I do hereby certify that the above is a true copy from said records. WITNESS my hand and the SEAL OF THE DEPARTMENT OF PUBLIC HEALTH at Boston on the date inscribed hereon:

DAFFY D. DUCK
Registrar

IT IS ILLEGAL TO ALTER OR REPRODUCE THIS DOCUMENT IN ANY MANNER

Here is a completed template ready to be placed in a photocopier's paper tray. Place it in the tray, and appropriately position the vital record of your choice or creation in the copy area. Practice first by placing several blank sheets of paper in the copier's paper tray. Make a small mark on a few sheets to determine whether birth certificate template should be fed in face up or face down.

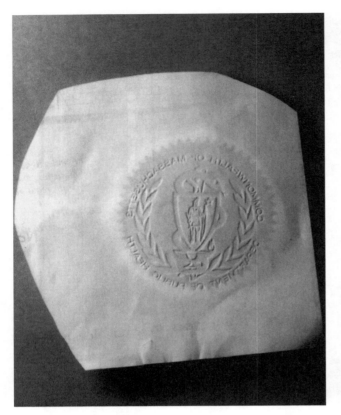

See? You were right. A depraved lunatic can make a great seal embosser using the Super Sculpey method.

dual citizenship and an Irish passport.[2] Motor vehicle registries in most states accept the long form as identification. The same type of form as a marriage or death certificate may also come in handy, especially when opening joint or estate bank accounts.

The Massachusetts long form is a typical example. An archived birth (or marriage or death) certificate is photocopied onto special copy paper. The special paper is really just plain copy paper with a heading and some official-looking red numbers at the top. The state's great seal is embossed over a green background at the bottom near a preprinted signature of the registrar. The special copy paper is placed into a photocopier so a congressman's niece can sell you "certified" copies at eight bucks a whack.

It's all ink and toner, baby, except for that nasty embossed seal.

If you've been reading this book's chapters in order, you may be thinking a depraved lunatic could readily replicate the state seal using the Super Sculpey method described in Chapter 5. The green background is only a minor problem. You can print it from just about any color printer. I'd prefer a laser or MD printer (Alps) printer to ensure that the ink won't run at an inconvenient moment. Green magic marker over a stencil would be a respectable "old school" approach.

But what about the vital statistics? The information contained in the birth record is entirely up to you. You can copy an existing record and ghost yourself in as is, or you can use Wite-Out and a matching typeface to change an existing record to something that better suits you. You could also make a record from scratch, though this would be much more involved. If you opt for the latter, be sure you have an actual record from the same year to use as a guide. Some bad people scan several records into their computer and then use PhotoShop to cut and paste together a composite record of their own Frankensteinian creation.

The above birth certificate abstract techniques can also be used to make firearm IDs, video store membership cards, employment badges, student IDs, and more. This is just a taste of what you can do at home. The following chapter delves into the more sophisticated techniques used to replicate state driver's licenses.

NOTES

1. "Year the record was supposedly made": this is a common mistake, though not a very critical one. Most clerks have no idea which styles were issued in which cities in which years. However, if you're going to take the time to copy a city's template, you may as well make sure the card style was used in the year your record was supposedly issued.
2. See previously mentioned *Identity, Privacy, and Personal Freedom: Big Brother vs. The New Resistance.*

Chapter 7

How Crooks Construct Kick-Ass Driver's Licenses

By the time some of you read this, the states below may have already changed their license format. As this is written, states are scrambling to keep one step ahead of document forgers (although I tend to think it's the other way around), and many new security devices are in the works. The feds are pushing Orwellian laws on the states, attempting to force the use of biometric identifiers on every state license. Digitized photos and fingerprints lurk just around the corner, my friends. What will ID forgers do then? We can only wait and see. This chapter shows what they're doing now. The techniques in this chapter will be useful to misanthropic motherfuckers for many years to come.

Even expired licenses have their uses. Since the expiration date on a driver's licenses only relates to one's legal driving status, many non-Orwellian establishments accept old licenses as ID. There are many places that have no established policy that a driver's license must be current. Often, it is up to the clerk whether to accept an outdated license as ID. Many liberal-minded people have no problem doing just that. If you aren't lucky enough to find liberal-minded people, apathetic and unobservant clerks are not in short supply. For various valid reasons, old IDs are often used to open bank accounts, establish mail drops, get library cards, and perform a host of other civic activities.

What are some valid reasons for having an expired driver's license?

- An elderly person stops driving so there's no point in renewing the license.
- You are diagnosed with a disease that precludes your driving (a medical bracelet or "dog tag" is convincing backup ID in these cases).

- A middle-aged man might say, "I stopped driving after my second heart attack—doctor's orders."
- A person on crutches or in a wheelchair might say, "As my MS progressed I saw no point in renewing my driver's license."
- A young person may say, "I was found at fault for a car accident in which my passenger—my best friend—was killed. I don't drive anymore."

These are just a few reasons that popped into my head as I was writing. I'm sure crafty con men have many more.

I'm equally sure those same crafty con men are well aware that many state "nondriver identification" cards are valid indefinitely. I have a friend with such a card from the 1970s. He still uses it today to cash checks. So you can see why this chapter's techniques will be in wide use for the next few decades.

We'll begin by outlining the basic procedure for constructing a novelty driver's license and then move on to procedures specific to a given state. This is the basic procedure for a standard laminated ID card–style license.

MINIMUM TOOLS REQUIRED

A very resourceful person can construct a novelty ID for nothing. You need not own any of the tools nor spend any money, provided you have access to the following:

- A computer running PhotoShop or comparable software
- A high-quality color printer
- A laminator
- The Internet

If it sounds like a lot to ask for, consider this. I can get in my truck right now, drive 4 miles to the local community college, sit in the library for a couple of hours, and walk out with a novelty ID ready for lamination. If you work in an office, you may have ready access to a laminator. If not, Kinko's, Copy Cops, Mail Boxes Etc., or a similar facility will do it for a buck or two.

Many public libraries these days—even in mid-sized towns—have rows and rows of computers with Internet access and graphics software networked to a color printer.

When sticky-fingered filchers live too far away from such valuable resources, they buy the necessary tools, make the IDs they need, and then return the goods to the store within 30 days for a full refund.

As you can see, there's more than one way to skin an ID.

BASIC PROCEDURE

We'll be discussing several different driver's licenses, each with its own distinct qualities. However, they share some basic construction steps. Rather than repeat the steps for each license, we'll outline them here and refer back as needed.

Obtain a Template

To make a novelty driver's license you'll need a template. If you've been with me since the beginning, you already know that a template is an actual-size computer image of the real license you'll be making, hopefully front and back. If you can't get the back, don't worry too much. I'll show you some stock backs that philandering phonies like to use.[1]

There are three ways to get a template for any given state.

- Design it yourself.
- Scan it into a computer.
- Download it from the Internet.

Design It Yourself

If you have great artistic skills, you can create the background and state logos using a sophisticated drawing program such as PhotoShop or Corel Draw. You can also stick with more traditional media, such as oil paints, colored pencils, or markers, and then scan your finished product into a computer to add text and a photo.

Some IDs are simple enough to copy even if you lack artistic skill.

Scan It into a Computer

If you have the actual license, you can scan it into a computer. If your final product will be printed out with an inkjet or laser printer, you'll need a minimum 600-dpi scan. If you're going to use a dye-sub printer, such as the Alps, you can get away with 200 to 300 dpi.

Download It from the Internet

The Internet is usually your best bet. Not only can you find abundant templates, but you can often get fully layered PhotoShop files that have already been reworked by someone. You need only add your photo and identifying information to the file and print it out. Usually, you'll have to trade something of equal value or pay a small premium to receive these files.

Do a Preliminary Printout

Once you have a template, print it out onto regular copy paper and verify its dimensions against an actual license or the actual-size pictures in the *I.D. Checking Guide.* Use a ruler that measures in millimeters or sixteenths of an inch. Keep all measurements within 1mm or 1/16 of an inch. Check the following:

- Height and width[2]
- Size of logo
- Position of all text boxes
- Distances between text lines
- Length of text lines
- Height of fonts
- Anything else that catches your eye

If you are using a JPEG image or a poorly reworked PhotoShop template, some or all of these measurements may be off. If so, make corrections in the following manner.

- Measure the height and width of the actual license.
- Resize the template using these dimensions. Do not change the aspect ratio; that is, checkmark the constrain proportions box.
- Recheck all of the above measurements.

Things may still be off at this point, but if you have the proper height and width, you can adjust everything else as you rework the template. Even when I have a template that is perfect, I redraw lines and retype text to eliminate fuzziness. You will absolutely need to do this when working from a plain JPEG image. If working from a layered file, you'll have to decide for yourself which elements need rework.

PHOTOSHOP 101: TEMPLATE ENHANCEMENT TRICKS

Whether you've designed it yourself, downloaded a JPEG image from the Internet, or finagled a layered PhotoShop document, your template will seldom be perfect. The following tricks will help you enhance even the worst JPEG image. This section will also serve as an introduction to PhotoShop for those who are unfamiliar with it.

Adjust Image Resolution

Since adjusting the dpi of an existing image really doesn't change its resolution, only do this if working with a particularly bad JPEG image in need of total rework. If this is the case, follow these steps:

1. Open JPEG image in PhotoShop.
2. Resize image to your target width and height, specifying at least 300 dpi.
3. Save the image as a PhotoShop document.
4. Now use this horrible image only as a guide for a complete redo. Call this layer "placement."
5. Start a new layer called "background."
6. Follow the remaining enhancement techniques given below.

The I.D. Checking Guide *is published and distributed by The Driver's License Guide Company. Other organizations have been known to distribute the guide. I got mine from the Florida Banker's Association. If you have trouble getting it, see Chapter 3 of my book* Identity, Privacy, & Personal Freedom: Big Brother vs. The New Resistance *for some tips on how to obtain it.*

Background Layer

Sometimes the background layer can look splotchy due to imperfections in the original document. In most cases you'll want to clean this up. Follow these steps:

1. Use the marquee tool to select the background area.
2. Use the eyedropper tool to pick up the average background color.
3. Use the paintbrush tool on its largest setting to repaint the selected area.

Repeat steps 1–3 above for all major background areas. Make sure you are reworking the correct layer.

Redoing Logos and Seals

Most driver's licenses contain the state's DMV logo or great seal, sometimes both. Pros isolate

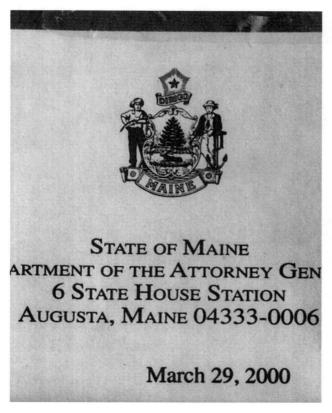

Need a seal? Write to the state and await a response. Here are the letterheads I got back after writing the Maine and Massachusetts state secretaries offices.

these images to their own layer. This is a problem if data fields overlap the image because it's difficult to select the image without selecting the data fields. Choosing Select, Color Range can sometimes solve this problem, but then white "holes" are left in the image where the data fields were. This is okay if you don't mind filling all the holes back in, which is exactly what many document forgers do.

Sometimes it's possible to delete a logo or great seal altogether and paste in a new one. To do this you'll need a good scan of the image, be it logo or seal. If it's a simple enough logo, like New Jersey's, you can draw it yourself.

Another alternative is to write your DMV/RMV/MVB (or whatever those bastards call themselves in your state). Make sure the letter requires a response. When they respond, scan the logo off their letterhead.

You can also visit your state's DMV on the Internet. Usually, you can find the logo at the top of the DMV's home page or embedded in the background somewhere. Systematically follow their links until you find a suitable image. Once found, right-click it. Select "Save Image As . . ." and save the image to your hard drive.

Visit www.state.YS.us, where "YS" is the two-letter abbreviation of your target state. You might find what you're looking for there. There is a virtual gold mine of symbols and seals at: http://www.netstate.com/states/symb/seals. Go hog-wild downloading state seals and spread them across the Internet before this site closes down.

Once you have the image, use PhotoShop to get it reworked, resized, and adjusted to the proper color and opacity. Here is an example.

Try this to correct fuzzy logos and seals:

1. Cut the logo from the background layer and paste it into its own layer called "logo."
2. Select the logo using the marquee tool.
3. Use the sharpen command (Filter, Sharpen from the main menu) and see if that improves the logo to an acceptable quality.

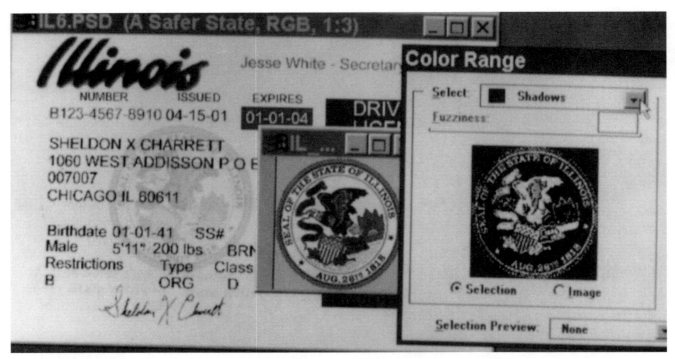

I downloaded the great seal of Illinois from the state's Web site, used the Select, Color Range function and selected "Shadows," which worked well enough for this seal of mostly dark colors. You may have to select colors individually when working with other seals. In the Select, Color Range dialog box, choose the eyedropper with the + symbol to keep adding colors until the entire seal is selected.

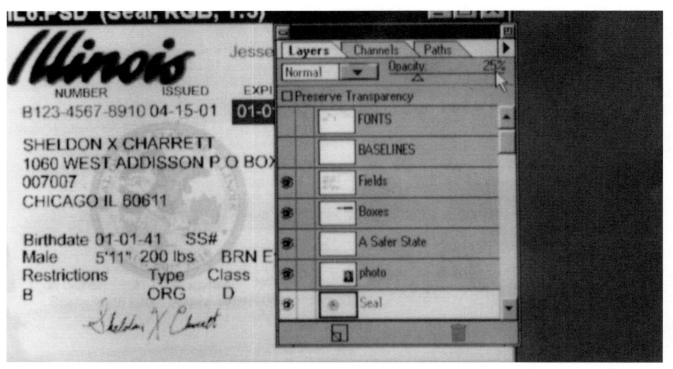

Once you've selected all the colors you want, copy and paste the seal into its own layer. Highlight the layer and select an opacity of 25 percent (actual opacity will vary depending on the ID).

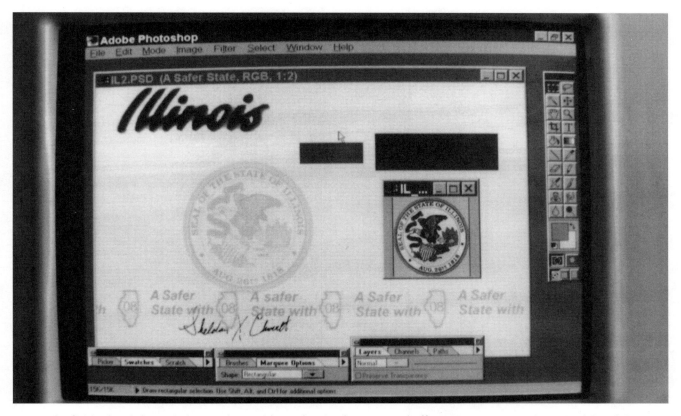

Here's the finished seal shown in its own layer with overlapping layers turned off. At 25-percent opacity, a 72-dpi Web image does the trick.

You can also clean up your logo or add detail to it by zooming in and using the paintbrush or pencil on its tiniest setting. To remove irregular specs and splotches from the edges, use the lasso selection tool, which allows you to select irregularly shaped areas. It's an odd tool to use at first, but once you get used to it, it can really work wonders.

If you're working from a previously reworked template, you may have a clean logo that is the wrong size or color. In this case, follow these steps:

1. Cut the logo and paste it into its own layer.
2. Resize it to the proper dimensions by choosing Effects, Scale.
3. Click Image, Adjust, Replace Color from the main menu to adjust the color of the logo.

Redo Fonts

There will be times when you'll want to redo the fonts on an ID template due to a bad scan. Matching fonts takes some practice. In most cases, you won't be able to find the exact font you need. You'll have to take pains to find a font that is the next best thing. Obviously, the closer the better.

But even when you find an acceptable font, there are a few more things to consider. Among these are the following:

*   Unusual characters
*   Character size
*   Character spacing
*   Line spacing

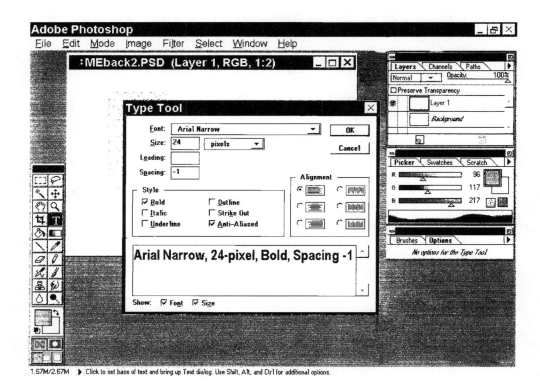

Character spacing can be stretched by entering a positive number in the Spacing box or compressed by entering a negative number. As illustrated, Arial Narrow, 24-pixel bold, with spacing set to –1 will match the font of a Maine license back.

Unusual Characters

No, not the ones you meet in Harvard Square or on Sunset Strip. I'm talking about fonts. Sometimes, even when you've found a pretty close match for a font, there is one character that's still unacceptable, usually because of some quirk that it has or doesn't have.

The best example I can think of is the dot matrix zero with a diagonal line through it. You see this character on state driver's licenses that have data fields filled in by a dot matrix printer. A good match for this font is called Bitmap. But the Bitmap zero doesn't have a line going through it. This is fine if you don't need a zero in your document, but what if you do?

This is really not a difficult problem to solve once you're aware of it. Diabolical dirtbag document forgers will go so far as to edit the font using a program such as Softy, the shareware birthchild of one Dave Emmett. Both Softy and Dave can be found at http://users.iclway.co.uk/l.emmett. If this address has changed by the time you read this, fear not. Softy is well documented on the Internet, and support sites should pop up in any search engine by entering the keyword "softy."

For us innocent folks who don't need to edit many fonts, it's a simple matter to draw a line over the zero using the PhotoShop line tool. Alternatively, you could paint in the line or other squiggle one pixel at a time after zooming in on the offending character (Ctrl +). Copy your special character and paste it wherever needed on your template.

Another good dot matrix font is called, well, Dot Matrix. Bitmap is better for a dense dot matrix effect, but Dot Matrix is better for sparse matrices (like those of the archaic 7-dot printers).

Character Size

You would think you could simply select the same font size the state uses, but even if you have this information, this is not always the case. Consider this: You go to the DMV and fill out a license information card. The information headings are in Courier 12 point—an easy font to reproduce. But then what happens? The information card is placed in a camera, where it is shot down to some wretched fraction of its original size. When felonious philanderers try to reproduce the license on a computer, Courier 12 point is way too big. So they try 10 point, which is still a bit too big. When they try 9 point, they realize it's too small!

Sometimes the difference is so small that it's not worth trying to fix. But other times, shyster charlatans insist on getting the font size exact. Fortunately, PhotoShop allows you to adjust the font size in terms of pixels, which gives you total control. If you find yourself between standard "point" sizes, adjust your font size in terms of pixels instead. Say Courier 9 point is equal to a setting of 20 pixels and Courier 10 point is equal to a setting of 30 pixels (not actual numbers, for example only). You can force a font size between 9 point and 10 point by selecting a pixel setting between 21 and 29. Using this technique, you can get your font sizes exact.

Character Spacing

Even after you've adjusted the font size you may realize that the space between characters still isn't quite right. Again, PhotoShop comes to the rescue.

Line Spacing

You can manually adjust line spacing by selecting the line with the marquee tool and sliding it up or down.

Character Size and Spacing

It is often useful to use PhotoShop's Scaling feature to simultaneously adjust character size and spacing. Get the font, character size, and spacing as close as you can by using the above techniques. Then use the following procedure to scale the text.

1. Select the text you wish to stretch or compress.
2. From the main menu choose Image, Effects, Scale.
3. Grab the corner square and pull down to adjust height. Drag the mouse very slowly. At first you'll see no progress; then the height will suddenly skip 3 pixels or so. Once this happens, slowly drag the mouse back 1 or 2 pixels to the size you want.
4. Hold cursor over the text and "hammer" it into place.

Enter Identifying Info

Once you have the data fields ready on the template, it's time to fill out the ID card. You should do this in another layer using the proper fonts. But . . . Which Fonts Do You Use? This is the $64,000 question of driver's license forgery. Decades ago, before the advent of holograms and bar codes, states used obscure fonts to thwart forgeries. Even though the desktop publishing revolution has dramatically simplified document forgeries, obscure fonts are still a hurdle for forgers. In many cases, you will not be able to match the font exactly and, even when you can, you will not exactly match its size.

Despite the seemingly infinite number of eventualities you have to concern yourself with, you need not feel overwhelmed. In many cases, others have done the work for you through repeated experimentation. For example, using 9-point Courier New Bold for the New Jersey driver's license is the closest you'll ever get to matching the font exactly. Pretty painless, huh?

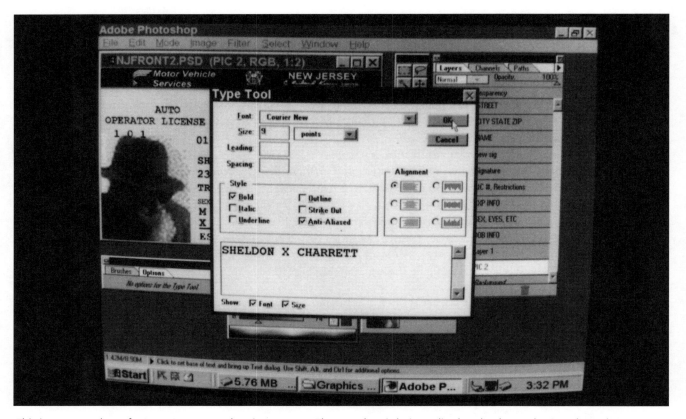

This is a screen shot of a New Jersey template in progress. The template is being edited and enhanced using PhotoShop 3.0. The New Jersey font scheme is pretty easy to remember: Courier New 9-point bold.

Asking around the Internet seems to be the best way to determine which fonts to use. Many times you can get someone to e-mail you a font that he's used successfully.

Ruthless, marauding, mobster-type ID forgers often use whatever font they have on hand that most closely matches. They know that clerks checking the ID will not notice if the font is off a little. Clerks are busy looking at the information on the card and seldom suspect that a well-made ID is a fake.

Some specific state driver's licenses are presented in the second half of this chapter. The information under each state will seem sparse compared to the detail presented up to this point. But finding the various fonts and font sizes for a specific state's driver's license is often the biggest part of the ID battle. It's something that keeps modern document forgers very busy. Therefore, each state listed in this chapter will have the proper fonts and sizes already calculated for easy academic experimentation. Anyone who has ever undertaken the task of font matching will appreciate the value of having this work done for them.

Dealing with Signatures

When applying for or renewing a license or ID, you are usually given a card to sign, which you sign, more often than not, in black ink. The clerk then does something mysterious with the card and takes your picture. After a little while, the clerk hands you a laminated ID card. It has your signature on it, but it is smaller than when you signed the card. This is mildly interesting to most people; then they stuff the ID in their wallet and never think again about how it was made.

The clerk photographed the information card with you standing next to it. Just like a vacation snapshot, the image in the picture is smaller than the actual object photographed. This presents a minor problem for ruthless reprobates who use the computer template method of forging driver's licenses. The template method does not involve shooting down the ID. You are left to choose between signing a printed template or importing your signature into PhotoShop. Each of these choices presents its own set of pros and cons.

Signing a printed template is difficult because (1) you have to write very small, and (2) the specially coated high-resolution papers are not friendly to ballpoint pens. Using a felt-tip marker causes smudge problems. The advantage to signing a printed template is that the signature—if you can get it done—looks more natural, less electronic.

Importing your signature into PhotoShop allows you greater control over how it looks and eliminates the possibility of ruining a printed template with a bad signature. The downside? The printed signature looks somewhat computerized. This, however, may not be a drawback for IDs with digitized signatures and is only a minor problem otherwise. To import a signature, use the procedure described in Chapter 6 under "Steal City Seal."

Printout and Finishing Touches

Once you have a complete template design most of the battle is over. It's mechanics and common sense from here on out. Some states will have the added hurdle of a particularly complex hologram, but by this point you will have already decided how to handle it (see Chapter 4).

Put simply, you print out the templates, front and back; put them together with a hologram; and laminate. Then there are a thousand subtleties one must keep in mind, depending on the style of license, type of hologram, intended use, etc. Most of the subtleties and pitfalls have been covered in this book and others, but here are a few checkpoints:

- Maintain the quality of the printout. Use correct photographic paper and printer settings.
- Choose the right type of paper and ink. Will you need a barrier layer to prevent bleeding?
- Keep edges clean and straight. It is best to glue front to back before cutting.
- Rounded corners must look professional! Keep at it till you get it right.
- If using a diffractive grating hologram, make sure it is protected from vinyl chloride in the lamination pouch.
- Do not overheat diffractive grating holograms.
- Use the correct thickness lamination pouch; go light if adding protective layers.

SPECIFIC INFORMATION BY STATE

Now that you know the basic construction procedures for state driver's licenses, I will present some specific information for a few select states. If you want to make an academic study of a state that I haven't listed, it is a simple matter to do the necessary research on your own and then apply the foregoing techniques. Even if you're not interested in any of the states below, you will pick up a pointer or two by studying them. The various fonts and sizes may be of particular value: I invested a considerable amount of time deciphering them.

New Jersey

The current New Jersey driver's license is the most faked ID of all time.[3] Even a real New Jersey driver's license is fast becoming useless as a means of "official" identification. It is the most widely faked because it is one of the easiest to reproduce. For this reason, many newbie forgers cut their teeth on it. Since New Jersey uses a metallic hologram, the following is also a good study for those who wish to learn how lawless cretins fake them.

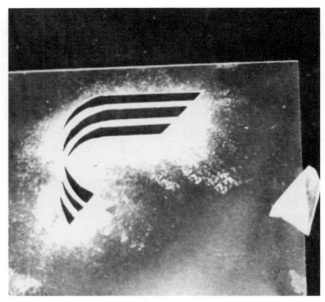

Make a stencil of the New Jersey logo out of Dura-Lar film.

Finished (modified and enhanced) New Jersey template printed from an Alps MD-5000 onto VPhoto print film. Save a copy as a high-quality JPEG. Import it into Word and then copy and paste the image to fill a page. Print it for experimentation.

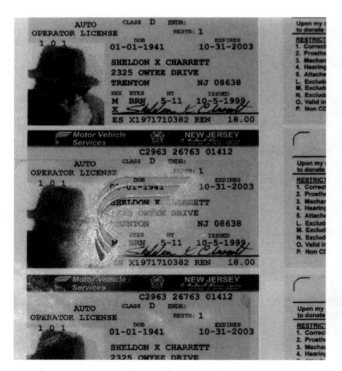

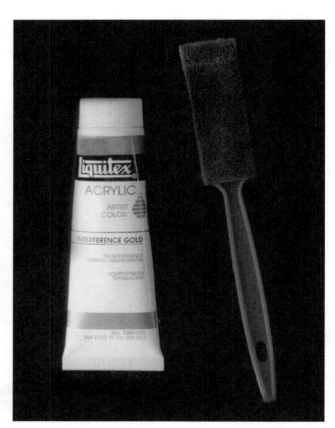

Lay the Dura-Lar stencil over the printed New Jersey template in the appropriate position.

You'll need Interference Gold acrylic paint and a foam applicator to complete this procedure. Astute forgers dab the applicator on tape to clean it before use. Any 2-inch cellophane tape should do the trick.

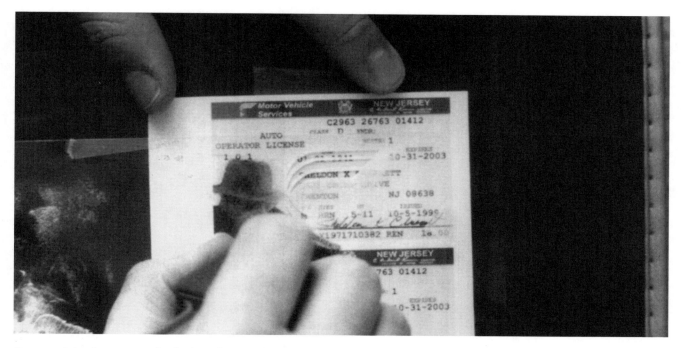

Press a miniscule amount of paint into the stencil. Jackhammer repeatedly until you feel you've covered the area completely. You won't be able to see the results until you remove the stencil and hold the template at an angle to the light. If you can see the results before this, you're probably putting on too much paint.

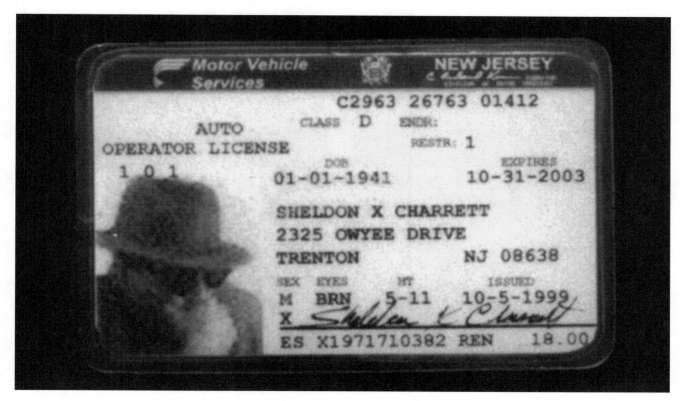

Front shot of finished product. Notice how you cannot see the hologram at this flat angle.

Angle shot of finished product to show Interference Gold hologram.

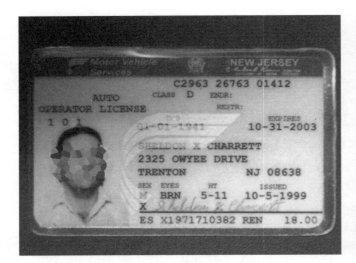

A Metallic Gold hologram printed with an Alps MD-5000 printer.

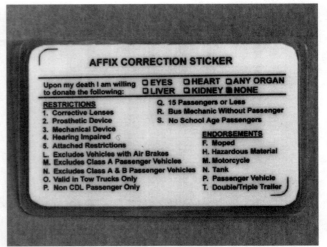

Photo showing back of finished product. Actual crooks remember to place an X in the box next to the "NONE" organ donation choice.

TABLE 2: FONT INFO FOR SOUTH DAKOTA	
Section	*Font*
FIELDS	Bitmap, 6-point, bold Upper case
VITAL STATISTICS DATA	Dot matrix, 6-point, bold. Doubled and offset 1 pixel to increase density Upper case
NAME AND ADDRESS	Dot matrix, 8-point, bold Doubled and offset 1 pixel to increase density Upper case
LICENSE NUMBER	Bitmap, 12-point, bold Upper case
...DAYS PRIOR TO EXPIRATION...	Bitmap, 5-point, bold Spacing = 1 Upper case
POWER OF ATTORNEY **LIVING WILL**	Dot matrix, 5-point
"WILLIAM J. JANKLOW, GOVERNOR" (May differ depending on year)	Dot matrix, 25-pixel, bold Spacing = .5

Specific Procedure: Obtain Template, Spruce It Up, Enter Info

Follow the basic procedure to obtain the template and modify it to an acceptable quality. Because this license is so widely faked, the Internet is abundant with templates. New Jersey has the simplest font scheme: use Courier New 9-point bold for your name, address, and all identifying information.

Well, there you have it: one of the most basic licenses there is. It makes a great study, but, again, don't try to use it anywhere. This one's so basic that, even legitimate New Jersey driver's licenses are rejected as proof of ID.

South Dakota

Nothing earth-shattering here: a simple rectangular hologram. The license term is up to five years and seven months, allowing for six-month early renewal and one-month grace period after expiration. Even if South Dakota changes this license format, the licenses will still be acceptable till at least 2004. Malicious mental defectives will be using this license for quite some time.

Maine

Remember the Maine! Er, I Mean, Why Maine?

The current Maine driver's license is the age-old basic laminated card with repetitive lettering. I commend the state for not going the way of Big Brother—at least not just yet. The problem is those damn pirates coming in off the high seas. They exploit this poor little license to fulfill their prurient pleasures with the fair maidens on dry land. And there's no end in sight. A Maine driver's license issued in 2000 is good until 2006. That means even in 2005, a pirate with a Y2K Maine ID can run around pillaging to his heart's content.[4] It just doesn't seem fair, does it?

Maine template. You do not have to worry too much about the corners or edges at this point. These will be trimmed in the final step.

Place template in typewriter and type away. Keep in mind that Maine has a seven-digit license number and a six-year term expiring on the applicant's birthday. Issue date may be before birthday.

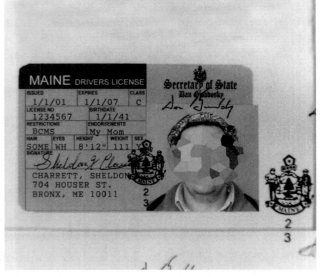

Place passport photo or other self-portrait in appropriate corner, overlay the seal/signature/camera number transparency, press it all together with a pane of glass, and take exposures from varying distances to ensure that you get a proper-sized print back from the developer.

The Maine license is one of only a handful remaining that can be produced entirely by old-school methods. I will use it to demonstrate a few such techniques.

"Hand-Drawn" Template

The Maine template is very basic. It can be drawn by hand or possibly made with transfer lettering. For our purposes, and because I am not a good drawer, the top photo on page 76 is actually a computer-generated template. But you can see where artistically inclined incorrigibles could readily draw this with pen and ink. Crooks with good Dumpster-diving skills could dig a blank information card from behind a Maine DMV. You might choose to use the template at the top of page 76 to aid your academic study of this license. You can photocopy the seal, signature, and camera number onto a transparency to make an overlay.

I've thoroughly covered this procedure in two other books, so I'm not going to rehash the details.[5] But here are a few important reminders. The photo at the lower right-hand corner of page 76 was shot with a 200mm macro lens. To get the end product the correct size, I had to shoot it fully zoomed out from about 20 inches away. Different macros with different settings and focal ratios will produce different results. The professional criminal must experiment on his own.

Security Pattern

The Maine driver's license has a repetitive security pattern on the lamination pouch. Fortunately for criminals, but unfortunately for law-abiding citizens who just read about criminals, this security feature is a simple "STATE OF MAINE" pattern repeated in a straight column down the face of the laminated card. It is a standard Interference Gold color and effect. Again, a gifted artist could spend a few hours painting this in, but here are a few alternatives for the semi-gifted, the not so gifted, and the just plain brain dead.

Rubber Stamp

For about $20 you can have a rubber stamp made up that says "STATE OF MAINE" in a repeated column. Order it from another state and the person you speak with will probably have no idea why you want it but will be happy to take your $20. Alternatively, you could buy a do-it-yourself stamp kit for around $10. I have such a kit, and the font just so happens to be the right type, although a bit bigger. I doubt most bureaucrats would notice a larger font.

Gently brush Interference Gold acrylic paint onto either type of stamp using a foam applicator. Use a miniscule, almost invisible amount. At this point you have several options:

- Stamp a piece of Dura-Lar film, which you'll later lay over the printed ID template before laminating.
- Stamp an ID already laminated with a 5-mil pouch and then relaminate with another 5-mil pouch.
- Stamp a heat-laminated ID and then "cold-laminate" it with Super Clear cellophane tape.
- Stamp a laminated ID and then heat-laminate just the front using half a 5-mil pouch.

Remember that the repetitive "STATE OF MAINE" pattern extends to the very edge of the ID (not just to the edge of the visible template). Sometimes you must tear the fused edge of a lamination pouch to achieve this effect.

Some disadvantages of the do-it-yourself kit are as follows:

- You have to assemble the letters "STATE OF MAINE" yourself.
- You have to stamp the lamination pouch several times.

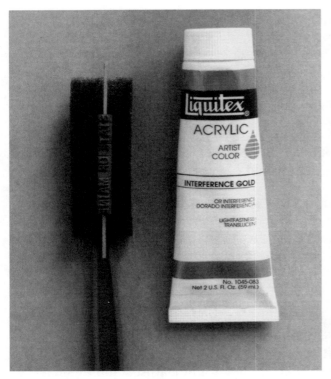

Do-it-yourself stamping kit. Arrange the letters to say "STATE OF MAINE." Use narrow spacers to minimize the length. The font is very close to the actual font used. Most bureaucrats won't notice the difference.

A mock-up printing press to transfer the repetitive pattern onto the lamination pouch or transparent insert. Rub only the slightest amount of Interference Gold onto the rubber stamp. If you make a mistake on one line, it's easy to erase it and redo.

- You have to keep reapplying the Interference Gold paint to the stamp.
- You have to be very careful to keep the repetitive pattern in line.

Once done, the letters are still slightly too big.

Another Repetitive Lettering Method

You can print the repetitive pattern onto Dura-Lar (or an even thinner transparent film) using a Metallic Gold cartridge in an Alps printer. Here's the procedure:

1. Open Word or another word processor and make 20 or more "STATE OF MAINE" lines.
2. Select all text and change to Arial 10-point font.
3. Change line spacing to .7. In Word choose Paragraph, Line Spacing, Multiple, and enter .7 into the box.
4. Select Print, Properties to get into the Alps control window.
5. Now, you have to cheat a little by telling the printer you are using laser printer paper. Then select Spot Colors, Single Ink, Metallic Gold, and choose OK.
6. Load a transparency, Dura-Lar, or other transparent film into the Alps and print.[6]

You now have a repetitive pattern in gold ink that is way too dark to be believable.

Get the cleanest, finest piece of steel wool you can find and begin to gently efface the repetitive pattern. If you see immediate progress, you're pressing way too hard. Ease off and take your time.

Repetitive lettering printed onto Dura-Lar and laid over a composite Maine ID card. Add a back, cut, and laminate for finished product.

RESTRICTION CODE

A -	CORRECTIVE LENSES
B -	DAYLIGHT OPERATION
C -	DRIVER IMPROVEMENT
D -	MOTORCYCLE
E -	MOTOR DRIVEN CYCLE
G -	GEOGRAPHICAL
M -	MEDICATION
R -	MOPED
Q -	CONDITIONAL LICENSE
S -	SPECIAL EQUIPMENT
W -	OPERATION OF VEHICLES EQUIPPED WITH AIR BRAKES NOT ALLOWED

ENDORSEMENT CODE

H -	HAZARDOUS MATERIALS
I -	MOTORCYCLE
J -	MOTOR DRIVEN VEHICLE
K -	VALID UNTIL 30 DAYS AFTER DISCHARGE FROM ARMED FORCES
N -	TANK VEHICLE
P -	PASSENGER (BUS) VEHICLE
T -	DOUBLE/TRIPLE TRAILER
X -	COMB. TANK HAZARDOUS MATERIALS
Y -	SCHOOL BUS OVER 15 PASSENGERS
Z -	SCHOOL BUS 15 PASSENGERS OR LESS INCLUDING DRIVER

PLACE ORGAN DONOR DECAL HERE

The actual text on the Maine license back is blue.

Work evenly on all parts of the repetitive pattern using a wide circular motion. After a while you'll begin to see the effect you're looking for. This is a crucial point because some areas will be more effaced than others. Once a letter is half erased, it does not take much to make it disappear completely. So now you have to be more selective with the steel wool. Gently rub only the areas that still need rubbing. Do not worry about the light scratches on the plastic (transparency, Dura-Lar, whatever). Those will be filled in by the vinyl chloride in the lamination pouch and will actually help keep air bubbles from forming.

You'll want to beat up the license a little when you're done. A supposedly four-year-old license is less believable if it is shiny and scratch free.

Another One

If the above repetitive lettering method sounds like more work than you want to get into, there is a much faster method. You can print directly to Dura-Lar or a transparency using a gold ink cartridge in an Alps printer as described above, with one minor adjustment. First select all the text and choose Format, Font. Next to Color, choose 25-percent gray. Now print.

The downside to this method is that the gold ink does not offer a continuous tone. Rather, it prints the repetitive pattern as a sparse series of dots. Upon close inspection, the dot pattern may look unnatural to a savvy clerk. This aside, I'd bet an otherwise well-made license using this repetitive lettering technique would work nine times out of ten in states other than Maine.

Choosing Outline under the Format Font menu results in a slightly different look (outline lettering), which also may work well in distant foreign states.

And Another One

If you want to experiment with various "shades" of gold, there is yet another variation on this theme. You'll recall that Word gives you little choice as to the "tone" of gold; you can

| TABLE 3: FONT INFO FOR MAINE ||
Section	Font
FIELDS	Arial Black, 5-point, bold Stretched vertically 1 to 2 pixels Compressed horizontal to actual width
DATA	Courier New, 8-point, bold Height stretched one or two pixels
SECRETARY OF STATE	Old English Text MT, 10-point, bold Stretched vertically 1 to 2 pixels and Compressed horizontally to same length as original
"DAN GWADOSKY" (May differ depending on year)	Old English Text MT, 7-point, bold Stretched vertically 1 to 2 pixels, Compressed horizontally to fit
CAMERA NUMBER	Courier New, 8-point, bold Stretched vertically 2 pixels

choose between 25 and 50 percent. The latter is way too dark for our purposes, so you really have no choice at all. While 25 percent seems to be just about right for Maine, you may desire to experiment with different gray-scale percentages when using this repetitive lettering technique, especially on other IDs.

Print out the repetitive pattern in black ink onto white laser printer paper and then scan the image back into your computer. This step ensures proper font size and letter spacing. If you were to capture the repetitive pattern directly from the screen, it would more than likely contain imperfections because even "true type" screen fonts are not so "true" once you play with character and line spacing. Now, import the scanned image into Word as a picture object and place the object in the header. Right-click the picture to edit its properties. Convert it to a "watermark" and then adjust the brightness and contrast to suit your needs. You can see where this gives you infinite control over the image's transparency.

If you have PhotoShop, you can also import the image into its own layer of a .PSD file. Once done, it is a simple matter to experiment with different opacities to adjust the transparency of the pattern.

None of these repetitive lettering methods is perfect. But if you remember to beat up your ID real good when it's done, it will be believable. Steel wool is a good tool for "aging" an ID. You can use the foregoing methods for any ID that has repetitive gold lettering.

Computer Template Method

The Maine license is a good candidate for old-school construction methods, but you can also make one using the computer template method. As I have provided for other states, here is the font information for doing just that.

Stretching and Compressing Text

Making a Maine driver's license template offers a glimpse at yet another of PhotoShop's powerful image manipulation routines. In Table 3 you'll note several instances where the text must be stretched or compressed. The actual term for this process is called *scaling*. Previously described text manipula-

TABLE 4: FONT INFO FOR MASSACHUSETTS	
Section	*Font*
FIELDS	Arial, 24-pixel bold italic, color white. Text placed inside solid black rectangles. Rectangle height is 2 pixels more than text, such that 1 pixel borders the white text on top and bottom. Upper case
COMMONWEALTH OF MASSACHUSETTS	Old English Text MT, 42-pixel, bold Title case
"DRIVER'S LICENSE" DATA	Dot matrix, 6-point Spacing = 1 Upper case
SIGNATURE BELOW	Arial, 20-pixel, italic Upper case
REGISTRAR	Technocrat, 4 point Text direction vertical. Once text is on screen, flip horizontal then vertical for proper orientation Very nice effect Upper case

tion methods can be used, but sometimes scaling the text is faster, more efficient, and better looking. See under "Character Size and Spacing" on page 69.

Using the Maine Template

You can print out the final template as a large card for a composite photo ID, or use PhotoShop to fill in the data fields and print it out as a small card ready for backing and lamination.

Maine Back

Just as they'll tell you in the back woods of Maine, there's more than one way to skin a cat—and they know firsthand, too. Well, I've already shown how a license back can be scanned into PhotoShop and reworked, or used as-is if it's a good scan. But some of the cleanest license backs are laid out with and printed directly from a good word processor. As previously mentioned, a word processor file takes up far less memory than a high-resolution PhotoShop or JPEG image. The Maine back shown on page 79 was mocked up in Word 97.

Massachusetts

This is a previous edition Massachusetts license, which was still valid in late 1998. With a five-year term, these suckers will be rearing their ugly heads well into the new millennium. The format shares many of the characteristics of several state nondriver identification cards, some of which are valid indefinitely. I chose this license for its intricate font variations, which by their sheer number once acted as a security feature. This was a great forgery deterrent in its day, but the illustration on page 82 shows how modern desktop publishing readily reproduces these fonts.

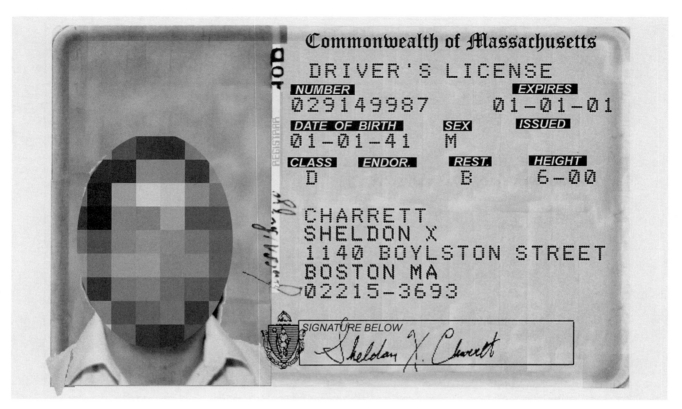

PhotoShop template of previous edition Massachusetts driver's license. Note that it uses five different fonts.

CLASS CODES

Class A: Any combination of vehicles with a gross combination weight rating GCWR of 26,001 pounds or more provided the GVWR of the vehicle(s) being towed is in excess of 10,000 pounds, except a School Bus.

Class B: Any single vehicle with a gross vehicle weight rating GVWR of 26,001 pounds or more, or any such vehicle towing another vehicle not in excess of 10,000 pounds GVWR, except a School Bus.

Class C: Any single vehicle that is less than 26,000 pounds GVWR, or any such vehicle towing a vehicle not in excess of 10,000 pounds GVWR, that is placarded for hazardous materials or designed to transport 16 or more persons, including the operator, except a School Bus.

Class D: Any motor vehicle or combination, except a Class A, Class B, Class C, Class M, or School Bus.

Class M: Motorcycle.

RESTRICTIONS			ENDORSEMENTS
B - Corrective lenses	G - Limit to daylight only	L - Vehicles without	H - Hazardous Materials
C - Mechanical aid	H - Limit to employment	Air Brakes	N - Tank vehicles
D - Prosthetic aid	I - Jr. Operator	M - Except Class A Bus	P - Passenger Transport
E - Automatic Trans	J - Other	N - Except Class A&B Bus	T - Doubles / Triples
F - Outside Mirror	K - CDL intrastate only	O - Except Tractor Trailer	X - Hazardous Material
			& Tank vehicles

OBTAIN CHANGE OF ADDRESS LABEL AT ANY REGISTRY AND ATTACH HERE WITH NEW ADDRESS.

As with the back of the Maine driver's license, the back of the Massachusetts license was also laid out with Word 97.

(A.)

CLASS 1 ALL VEHICLES NOT EXCEEDING 24,000 LBS. GVW. EXCEPT MOTORCYCLES
CLASS 2 INCLUDES CLASS 1 AND SINGLE VEHICLES EXCEEDING 24,000 LBS. GVW. EXCEPT
         MOTORCYCLES
CLASS 3 INCLUDES CLASS 1, 2 AND ALL VEHICLE COMB. EXCEEDING 24,000 LBS. GVW
         EXCEPT MOTORCYCLES
CLASS 4 MOTORCYCLES
CLASS 5 MOPED

A CORRECTIVE LENSES	E NEIGHBORHOOD ONLY	J AUTOMATIC TRANS.
B SPECIAL RESTRICTED*	(10 MI. HOME)	K POWER STEERING/BRAKES
C NO INTERSTATE DRIVING	F PREVIOUS DUI	L OTHER
D NOT TO EXCEED 50 MPH	G HAND CONTROLS	M OUTSIDE MIRROR
	H STEERING KNOB	N TURN SIGNALS

B* SPEC. REST. (Age 15) MAY OPERATE 6 a.m. to 6 p.m. EXCEPT FOR DAYLIGHT SAVINGS
    TIME 6 a.m. to 8 p.m. thur 8-31. 6 p.m. TO 6 a.m. ACCOMPANIED BY LICENSED DRIVER
    OVER 21 OR LICENSEE'S PARENT OR GUARDIAN. FARM MACH. OR EQUIP (OTHER
    THAN PASS. VEH.) MOTORCYCLES OF 6 BHP OR LESS AT AGE 16 BECOMES REG.
    LIC. AND DOES NOT HAVE TO BE EXCHANGED UNTIL EXPIRATION.

(B.)

THIS IS A LEGAL DOCUMENT UNDER THE UNIFORM
ANATOMICAL GIFT ACT OR SIMILAR LAWS
I hereby make an anatomical gift, effective upon my death

| | Any organ or tissue   DATE _____
| | Only the following
Signature of donor _____
WITNESS _____
WITNESS _____

Blood Type
RH Factor
Medical
Information /
Living Will
Seal Area

Class   Single Veh GVWR 16000 or Less Except Cycles
Restrictions   B —Corrective Lenses

(C.)

This card is the official verification of your Social Security number.
Please sign it right away. Keep it in a safe place.

Improper use of this card or number by anyone is punishable by fine,
imprisonment or both.

This card belongs to the Social Security Administration and you must
return it if we ask for it.

If you find a card that isn't yours, please return it to:
Social Security Administration
P.O. Box 17087, Baltimore, MD 21235

For any other Social Security business/information, contact your
local Social Security office. If you write to the above address for any
business other than returning a found card, it will take longer for us
to answer your letter.

Social Security Administration
Form SSA-3000 (4-90)   D12345678

Various ID backs: (A.) 1990 South Carolina driver's license; (B.) 1999 Illinois driver's license; (C.) a Social Security card, which crooks often find handy; and (D.) a generic card back you can modify to your heart's content. If you download a backless template from the Internet (an annoying reality, I'm afraid), try using one of these backs in its place. Modify them as you see fit.

1 2345 00000 0000

(D.)

ID BACKS

If you've ever scoured the Internet for high-quality driver's license templates, you know how frustrating it can be to find them. Many people end up paying for them and are still disappointed. It's even more frustrating when a good template does not include the back side! I find this exceedingly odd since one of the first things any decent ID checker does is turn the card over; sometimes this is the *only* thing a clerk does to verify an ID. I often wonder what people do when they get Internet templates without backs. I sometimes envision their finished product with a Mickey Mouse, Goofy, or Donald Duck sticker on the back.

Here are some license backs that can be used as generic backs for various state licenses when you can't find the right one.[7]

BUYING FAKE DRIVER'S LICENSES

Iniquitous inveiglers have recently learned that the Internet is one of the best places to buy such fake ID as state driver's licenses. Unfortunately these Internet sites are short-lived. The proprietor of www.youneedone.com recently met with a considerable amount of inner-party unpleasantness. For about $50, the man, whom I shall call Crett Barreras, would make you a top-quality driver's license from any state, perfectly replicating even the most intricate credit card–style driver's licenses with complex repetitive rainbow holograms.[8] The problem for diabolical dirtbags: Crett is now in the midst of a crushing lawsuit and has had his site forced out of operation.

So what's an anarchist to do? Play "Beat the Feds," that's what. Find the Web sites of other "Cretts" before the government does. Use search engines, join newsgroups, ask questions. You'll find what you're looking for before too long.

What about non-computer-savvy anarchists? Er, the old standbys I suppose will do. I won't list them all, but you know . . . Blue Hill Ave., Sunset Strip, Alvarado Street, Bonanza Road. You know which cities. If you don't, drive some night to the biggest city in your state and walk around till you hear someone scream, "Oh, my god, I'm being stabbed to death!" Walk toward the screaming—the gunshots should get louder; the body count should increase. Walk right to the center of the mayhem: that's where you begin your search.

I hope you understand why I can't list exact addresses. I want to keep the Crett Barrerases of the world out of prison if I can at all help it. Okay, now wait, I seem to hear a collective shout of *Why? Aren't the Crett Barrerases the very cretins this book is supposed to expose?* Well, that's really beside the point. I just happen to believe that prisons are best suited for violent offenders.

NOTES

1. Smart criminals never use an improvised ID back in the state that supposedly issued it.
2. This is width and height of the ID card, not the lamination pouch.
3. At the time of this writing.
4. It is possible that Maine could do a "recall" of all licenses and force citizens to upgrade to a more secure document. I tend to doubt this would ever happen, though. It would cost millions of dollars to implement, and the freedom-minded folks of rural Maine would oust every incumbent politician in the next election.
5. Charrett, *The Modern Identity Changer: How To Create and Use a New Identity for Privacy and Personal Freedom*, and *Identity, Privacy, and Personal Freedom: Big Brother vs. The New Resistance*, both available from Paladin.
6. Incidentally, you could print this onto paper with black ink as photo-ready artwork for a rubber stamp.
7. In this case you'd only use the ID in a state well distanced from the state that supposedly issued it.
8. It is important to note that Crett made his licenses using the techniques and equipment discussed in this book. Granted, his techniques were well refined and his business allowed him to spend thousands of dollars on the very best equipment, but the fundamental construction principles are the same.

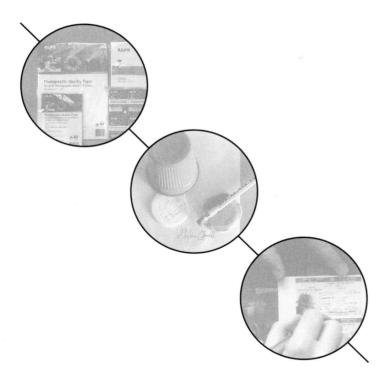

Conclusion

I have done my best to illustrate the various methods good-for-nothing bastards use to create false identification. I have demonstrated some of the most modern techniques—a few of which have hitherto escaped publication, and one of which was my very own creation. I have also expanded upon methods previously published by others and myself. And, for what it's worth, I've been told that I have given the world more synonyms for the word "crook" than it could ever need, want, or use.

Uh oh, there's that collective shouting again . . . *Hey, Sheldon, you never answered our question. Isn't this book about how naughty, nasty incorrigible anarchists spatter their wickedness onto our otherwise decent and pure society? Isn't it about staying as far as possible away from this evil? About renouncing Satan and the Hell's Angels he has deployed on our good earth to tempt us? Isn't this book about exposing the Crett Barrerases of the world so that we may be saved? You just brushed off that question at the end of Chapter 7. What's gives?*

Okay, okay. You got me. As far as the foregoing being what this book is really all about, to all my beloved readers, some of whom are federal agents in charge of a rather bulky dossier with my name on it, I have only this to say.

Peace.

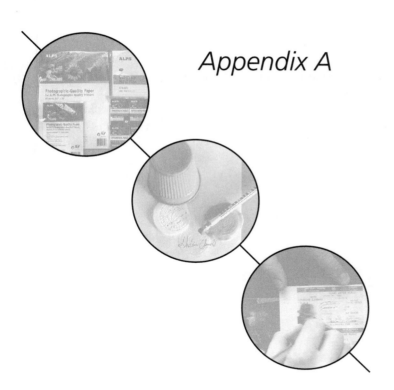

Contacting the Author

The only way to reach me is through the Internet at sxcharrett@yahoo.com. I know, in the past I've said I could be reached by writing to me in care of Paladin Press, but life has gotten too complex for this. The Internet is just too darned efficient, and I find I must take advantage of it before Big Brother ruins it with regulation.

If you have any questions, please first check my Delphi discussion board. If you do not find your answer there, please post a message in the appropriate category or create a category of your own, so that others my benefit from the ensuing discussion. The discussion board currently has a small user base, but I'm hopeful that it will grow after this book's publication. This is important because I've been getting more and more skittish about answering questions. The feds have tried on more than one occasion to trap me into an aiding and abetting rap with trick questions from my "readers." Although I will continue to answer *hypothetical* questions on my discussion board, eventually I hope that my readers will be able to share information among themselves. Hell, I might even learn a new trick or two, which might prove useful when I, too, am pressured by Big Brother into pulling the big Houdini.

You can find additional information as well as updates and corrections to all my books on my Web site:

http://www.phreak.co.uk/sxc

This site is graciously donated by the wonderful beings of the Phreakiverse. There are no annoying banners or pop-up ads. It is a truly philanthropic venture to support weirdos like me. When you visit my Web site, please also visit the rest of the Phreakiverse. You won't be disappointed. Please remember to thank the Webmasters for providing this much-needed service.

Since my current Web space is donated, it could disappear without warning if the Phreakiverse loses its funding. So, if you cannot find me there, please go the author links section of Paladin's Web site to find my new cyber locale:

http://www.paladin-press.com/authorlinks